STRAIGHT TALK:
The Power of Effective Communication

RIA STORY

CONTENTS

DEDICATION

This book is dedicated to my incredibly patient "editor,"
without whom I would not have gotten through English 101 in
college, much less have written this book. Mack Story is the
best connector I have ever seen, met, or heard about.
So, I married him.

A NOTE FOR READERS…

I consider it a privilege to help you improve your conversation, connection, and communication skills. There are many books on this subject, and I am humbled you chose to read this one. I sincerely believe you will find value in the skills, principles, and stories I have shared. I wrote this book because I believe I should "be a river" and pass on knowledge to others. The concepts I have learned, applied, and shared in this book have the ability to change your life.

They certainly changed mine.

CHAPTER ONE
THE POWER OF CONNECTION

"Communication - the human connection - is the key to personal and career success."

~Paul Meyer

I was nearly 20 years old before I realized I liked people. I never considered myself to be an "introvert" although most people would have. I simply didn't talk to people. Ask me a question, and you would get a monosyllabic response that discouraged any further dialogue. It's not that I didn't want to talk or communicate with people – I simply didn't know how.

I grew up very isolated, living on a farm in the middle of the woods. I was homeschooled. We didn't attend church regularly, and my social contact growing up was mainly limited to field trips with other homeschoolers. In the early 1980's in Alabama, opportunities for homeschooled children to participate in extra-curricular activities were limited, and my parents didn't pursue most of them.

I was also sexually abused by my father from age 12 – 19. Growing up with feelings of shame, guilt, hurt, and unworthiness only compounded my natural tendency to be withdrawn, even after I left home at 19. I share more about my story in some of my other books, *Ria's Story From Ashes To Beauty* and *Beyond Bound and Broken: A Journey of Healing and Resilience*.

Leaving home without a job, a car, or even a high school diploma, I got a crash course on the need for communication in "normal" society.

At 19, I had a great education, ability to think critically, reasoning skills, proactive attitude, and willingness to work hard. What I didn't have was the critical ability to connect with other people and communicate *effectively*.

Since I didn't have a GED or a high school diploma, finding a way to make a living wasn't going to be easy, but I was determined to start making money and earning my way.

My first job was working as a server at a pizza restaurant. I worked the lunch shift, Monday through Friday every day, from 11:00 – 2:00. Most customers would have the all-you-can-eat pizza and salad buffet because it was fast and didn't cost too much.

I was the only lunch server for all 36 tables in the restaurant. My job was to set up the buffet, keep the salad bar stocked and clean, make the tea, fill the ice bin, stock the soda machine, answer the phone, take delivery orders, greet the customers when they entered, take and fill their drink orders, keep dirty plates bussed, refill their drinks, check them out at the cash register, clean the tables, chairs, and floor after the customer left, wash all the dishes, put them away, and restock everything before I left. All for $2.13 per hour, plus any tips I made.

The lunch buffet was $5.99, and a drink was $1.35. Most customer bills came to less than $8.00 for lunch. The average tip is 10% for a buffet, so the best tip I could expect would be about $1.00 – and that's if I hustled really hard to keep their soda refilled and the dirty plates bussed. If I was too busy and the customer ran out of tea, I may not have gotten a tip at all.

I learned quickly that being an "introverted" waitress wasn't going to work. If I didn't smile at the customers, they thought I was unfriendly. If I didn't greet them enthusiastically, they didn't feel welcome or appreciated. If I didn't remember the names of the regular customers and what they liked to drink, they often wouldn't even leave me the change from their dollar.

I learned a lot of things during my years of waiting

tables, off and on earlier in my career. You see the best and the worst of people when you wait tables. But, the most important lesson I learned was to take initiative and connect with my customers. **Communicating information wasn't enough. I had to connect with them.** I could tell them where to get a plate and take their drink order, but how I did it made all the difference in whether they left me anything at all, or sometimes, several dollars.

What I want to share with you in this book are some of the lessons I've learned about connecting with people and communicating effectively. There aren't any shortcuts to success, but I hope I can help you avoid the detours and map out a faster route.

Effective communication skills are critical to our success in life.

On the professional side, the ability to communicate and relate to customers, co-workers, employees, or your boss can determine your career potential and define your success.

On the personal side, communication with your spouse, children, parents, and friends will determine your satisfaction in life (at least some of it) and define your relationships.

Regardless of your preferred personality style, or whether you consider yourself an introvert or extrovert, dealing with other people is a fact of life. Almost any situation you can think of requires you to come in contact and interact with other people sooner or later.

Your eye color cannot be changed. Your genetic ability to run a four-minute mile cannot be changed. Your ability to communicate CAN be changed. **Communication is a skill anyone can learn, and everyone can learn to do it better.**

CHAPTER TWO
CONNECTION IS CRITICAL TO COMMUNICATION

"Words - so innocent and powerless as they are, as standing in a dictionary, how potent for good and evil they become in the hands of one who knows how to combine them."

~Nathanial Hawthorne

I didn't get good at communicating and connecting with people overnight. I learned gradually over the next seven or eight years, after my first waitressing job, to get better at connecting and communicating and began to have moderate success as I developed my professional career. In order to earn several degrees, I went to college at night and worked two jobs, sometimes seven days a week. I slowly advanced in my career, somewhat limited by my lack of "people skills."

In February 2008, I started a new job at a hospital and was given the opportunity to attend leadership development courses. I wanted to take advantage of every opportunity to improve myself. I knew these courses would help.

I attended a short, four hour personal development class that opened my eyes to the concept of personal growth and intentional development. I wasn't accidentally improving anymore. Now, I was on an intentional growth mission.

I enrolled for every class offered from then on, and even looked for opportunities outside of what the hospital offered. In May of 2008, I bought my first leadership book, *"Leadership Gold"* by John C. Maxwell.

I started intentionally learning and developing my leadership skills and realized I could learn the language of influence to become more effective in every area of my life, personally and professionally.

The effect was transformational. In the past, I had

been afraid to start a conversation with a stranger. Today, I'm a full time speaker and author. I talk to thousands of people, blog regularly, and I even have an Instagram account. I'm about as social as you can get!

Think about some of the more impactful speakers you have seen or watched on TV. What made them memorable? What did they do or say to keep the attention of the audience? They didn't just stand up and talk – they connected with the audience first. How they do that varies from speaker to speaker, but what they all have in common is that the greatest speakers intentionally connect with the audience first.

Les Brown is one of my mentors and his ability to connect with an audience is outstanding. One of the ways he connects with the audience is to ask a volunteer to come up on stage with him. Then, he asks their name. Let's assume they reply "Jane." Les immediately creates an effortless connection to the audience using Jane's name.

Les says, "J stands for JUST DO IT, and Jane does exactly that. She makes things happen! A stands for ATTITUDE, and Jane has an incredibly positive attitude even in the face of adversity. She is always smiling and grateful! N stands for NEVER GIVE UP, and Jane never quits! She is determined, resilient, and strong! E stands for Everyone needs ENCOURAGEMENT, and Jane lifts up the spirits of everyone around her! She is a joy to be around and brings hope to others!"

Wow – he has just connected to everyone in the room by engaging their subconscious mind. Everyone in the room immediately starts to think of their own name and wondered what he would say about their "letters," or they began making up something themselves. Either way, it's a brilliant way to connect.

Les Brown's method of connecting may not work for you and odds are the majority of your connecting happens one on one, not from a stage in front of thousands of people. And, that's okay. It's important to find your own ways to connect to others. How you do it is not important. Doing it is what matters.

This concept applies not only to public speakers – it's equally important for the rest of us in our day to day interactions with others. The ability to connect first makes all the difference in how, or if, your message will be received.

Those who learn to connect and to do it well will be successful in life, at work, at home, and in relationships. Those who do not connect well will stumble around as I did when I first started waiting tables.

Even today, I'm not where I want to be in terms of my ability to connect. But, now that I've learned how important it is to connect, I work at it every day. Each and every interaction with someone is an opportunity to improve my skills by making sure they know I care about them as a person.

It requires some thought and certainly more energy to try and intentionally connect with someone. When you connect, your relationship will immediately improve with that person. Your communication skills will improve exponentially. And, your influence will increase.

My success, personally and professionally, is based on my ability to connect and communicate.

And, so is yours.

CHAPTER THREE
CONNECTION MULTIPLIES COMMUNICATION

"Communication leads to community, that is, to understanding, intimacy and mutual valuing."

~Rollo May

Communications of every kind bombard us. Billboards, radio ads, Facebook News Feed, people talking, co-workers complaining, children fussing, phones ringing, TVs blaring, and on and on. I read that on average, we are exposed to 35,000 messages of some type each day. That's an incredible amount of communication – and it's little wonder our brain tries to filter out the "noise" in an effort to focus on the important. There would be no way to effectively deal with and respond to each of those 35,000 messages.

Your brain works much like the spam filter on your email, by automatically sliding some messages to the side in order to deal with the ones that don't appear to be junk.

That works very well until we realize that sometimes we are part of the "noise" other people are tuning out.

Each of us wants to communicate. We want someone to hear and acknowledge our communications, because they are important to us. However, a huge challenge is to communicate in such a way that your message doesn't become just another piece of the clutter.

In order to communicate, we must be sure we are connecting. If we are connected, communication will be much easier and effective. If we are disconnected, it doesn't matter what we are communicating because the message isn't getting through.

Last year, Mack and I were invited to the corporate headquarters of Chick-fil-A to sit at a leadership roundtable with a couple from Belarus. This couple founded a leadership university in their home country and were visiting the U.S. and Chick-fil-A in order to seek advice on growing their program and teaching leadership on a larger scale to the people of Belarus. Mack and I were included because of our expertise teaching and speaking on leadership.

The couple had an incredible testimony of overcoming many hardships in order to be successful, but they were excited to be making an impact in the lives of the people who attended their university.

Since they did not speak English, and we do not speak Russian, communication was limited to what could be accomplished through an interpreter.

It's incredible how much you can communicate even when you don't speak the same language, as long as you are able to connect. The language barrier was there, but it was insignificant when compared to our mutual passion for helping people through leadership principles and our joy over connecting with one another.

We shared a meal, swapped stories, and even prayed together, and much of our communication was accomplished without words the other could understand. It didn't matter. We were connected at the heart.

Emotional connections can be formed in an instant, or they may take time to establish. Regardless of how quickly connections are formed, when they are established, communication becomes almost effortless.

Think of a connection as a multiplier for your communication skills. If your *communication* skills are a level 8 on a scale of 1 – 10, and your *connection* skills are a level 2, your effectiveness as a communicator will never be higher than a 16 out of 100.

However, if your *communication* skills are a level 6, but your *connection* skills are a level 8, your effectiveness as a communicator will be 48 out of 100. If you improve your connection skills, your effectiveness as a communicator will improve tremendously.

I've learned and applied the skills and concepts you will learn in this book. I know they are powerful. And, I also know they will work, if you apply them. They won't do you any good if you read about them and don't use them. Like any good tool, the tools in this book are only helpful when used.

Making changes in our communication style isn't easy. Anytime we are learning to improve ourselves, it will require effort, energy, and a commitment to operate outside of our comfort zone.

You won't get it right all the time. I know I don't. There are still times when I want to smack my forehead in frustration for saying the wrong thing or saying it the wrong way. At best, when that happens, I learn from it, so I don't repeat the mistake.

As you decide where you need to improve, make a commitment to work on just one thing during the first week or two. Start small and be intentional about when, where, and how you want to apply what you learn. Work at it, and then after a week, add something else or work to apply the skill in different situations. As time passes, you will realize a transformation is happening – but it won't happen overnight.

It's not easy. It's not fast. But, it's worth it. Communication and connection skills are indeed powerful for those who know how to use them.

Now, let's learn how.

CHAPTER FOUR
ATTITUDE IS EVERYTHING

"For success, attitude is equally as important as ability."
~Walter Scott

Attitude is the one thing that changes everything, even your ability to connect with others. I don't mean your attitude on the days things are going right. I mean your attitude each and every day, even when things aren't going your way. Your attitude reveals all someone needs to know about your character. If you are positive, it will show. If you are negative, it will also show. And, whether you have a positive or a negative attitude often determines your success.

Your attitude will affect both your feelings and your actions.

I was working as a waitress at a steakhouse many years ago. Waitressing was a side job for me at the time, on top of my full time job and night classes two nights a week. There were plenty of days when it was tempting to have a bad attitude or simply an uncaring attitude when I was very tired. I realized however, my attitude affected how people responded to me.

One Saturday night, I got a large table of ten people in my section. Since it was Saturday, the kitchen was running behind. When the party ordered appetizers, I rushed to place the order with the kitchen. Fast service meant a bigger tip, and I was working hard with a smile.

In the back, the appetizers came across the hot food line, and I loaded up my serving tray with a platter of golden fries covered with bacon and cheese and a bowl of ranch dressing on the side. With a stack of appetizer plates, it was a pretty full serving tray.

I lifted the tray to my shoulder and grabbed a tray stand on my way out the door. As I left the kitchen, I noticed one shoe felt loose, but decided to ignore it since I had my hands full as I moved through the restaurant.

I almost made it.

Less than ten feet from my table, the shoelace that came untied found its way under my other foot. As I firmly placed that foot down, and lifted the other, the issue became very clear, very fast.

It's easy to have a good attitude when things are going your way. It's so much more difficult to have a good attitude when you come crashing to the floor in a pile of cheese fries, ranch dressing, and broken appetizer plates. Right then and there, I had a choice.

That could be the worst waitressing moment of my life. Or, it could be the best. It was all in how I chose to look at it. I got up and firmly decided to smile – disregarding the ranch dressing dripping down my shirt!

I decided to laugh and smile about it, even though I was sure my table was going to be upset because those were clearly their cheese fries on the floor. But, they responded with a good attitude and very patiently waited for their food.

Our attitude about what happens to us is important. Our attitude towards other people is even more important.

If you carry with you an attitude of positivity and hope, people will want to be around you. If you carry an attitude of negativity and complain, people will not want to be around you. John C. Maxwell calls it the elevator principle, where you either lift people up or take them down. He says, *"People may hear your words but they feel your attitude."* Make it a point to always lift people up.

I can't talk about attitude without talking about Nick Vujicic.

Nick suffers from a rare disease that caused him to

be born without arms or legs. And yet, he hasn't let that stop him. As a teenager, he became inspired to be a motivational speaker. Today, he travels the world speaking about attitude, life without limits, and his faith.

Nick manages to live a full life, perhaps more so than even some completely "normal" people. He swims, surfs, plays golf, and even rides a skateboard.

Because of his "disability," Nick suffered from more than the usual teasing in school. He was bullied, made fun of, and suffered from depression at a young age.

What is most impressive is that through it all he has remained resilient. Regardless of his physical circumstances, he brings an attitude of hope and inspiration to everyone he meets.

We all have a story. Most people don't see it when they look at us. They don't know if you had a rough morning getting the kids to school on time and ran out of gas on the way. They don't know if you are having a difficult time in your marriage. They don't know if you are worried about a parent with cancer.

Regardless of what's going on in your life, you have the ability to choose a positive attitude.

Those who choose to do so, will be a light in the lives of others. People will naturally be drawn to them.

Attitude is a choice. It's not an easy choice some days. But, it is a choice every day.

Nick Vujicic said it best, *"Often people ask how I manage to be happy despite having no arms and no legs. The quick answer is that I have a choice. I can be angry about not having limbs, or I can be thankful that I have a purpose. I choose gratitude."*

CHAPTER FIVE
CAN YOU HEAR ME NOW?

"Any problem, big or small, within a family, always seems to start with bad communication. Someone isn't listening."

~Emma Thompson

Listening is the greatest communication tool to use when you want to connect with someone.

However, it's also the most difficult one to use because truly listening to someone requires complete attention. There are different levels of listening, and we have all been guilty of listening on a very shallow level at times. For example, when your three year old daughter is chatting on and on endlessly about her favorite Disney movie, you may tune out as your mind starts to plan what's for dinner. Or, your next-door neighbor fills your ears for 30 minutes talking about his new lawn care program, and you start to think about your big project coming due at work.

Frequently, when we are in a conversation, we listen only halfway and spend our energy thinking about what our response will be as soon as there is a chance to jump in and talk. We appear to be politely listening, but in reality, our mind is occupied with something else.

When we listen deeply to the other person, we are listening to the words they say, and the words they don't say. We are listening to the feelings they are expressing.

We may even reflect the feeling or paraphrase the content to demonstrate understanding. Listening requires our full and complete attention, focused eye contact and/or body language. Once you are sure the other person feels heard and understood and you are sure you understand, then it's okay to respond.

Anytime I am fully listening to someone, I don't need to think about how to communicate because they have my attention. It simply happens. I put down the phone or turn away from the computer. I turn my body toward the person who is talking with me and look directly at them to demonstrate they have my full attention.

I can always tell when someone doesn't really get listened to very often. They aren't sure how to respond when I focus on them and fully listen. When we make the effort to really listen deeply to someone, we are giving them the emotional space to express themselves to us.

Every one of us enjoys the attention from the people we love and those who love us. We crave it. Think of the four year old little boy who wants mom or dad to watch every thing he does. "Look Dad, watch me!" he cries out each time he jumps off the tire swing, again and again.

Listening is a great way to demonstrate you care because it does take intentional time and effort. It's a gift you can give to the person you are listening to. They don't have to wonder if they are being listened to.

Terry Felber, shared a memorable example of listening in his book, *Am I Making Myself Clear?* He states, *"The story is told of Franklin Roosevelt, who often endured long receiving lines at the White House. He complained that no one really paid any attention to what was said. One day, during a reception, he decided to try an experiment. To each person who passed down the line and shook his hand, he murmured, 'I murdered my grandmother this morning.' The guests responded with phrases like, 'Marvelous! Keep up the good work. We are proud of you. God bless you, sir.' It was not till the end of the line, while greeting the ambassador from Bolivia, that his words were actually heard. Nonplussed, the ambassador leaned over and whispered, 'I'm sure she had it coming.'"*

I have no idea of how accurate that story is, and I find it easy to believe it is slightly exaggerated. However, it makes the point – we often don't really listen. We hear what we are expecting others to say. We put our response on autopilot and dedicate our attention to something else.

Listening is so important in communication that Dr. Stephen R. Covey included it in his book *"The 7 Habits of Highly Effective People."* Habit 5 is *"Seek First To Understand, Then To Be Understood."*

How many misunderstandings could we avoid if we always tried to listen and fully understand the perspective of the other person before sharing our opinions, thoughts, and feelings.

In order to listen however, we must first be silent. The problem is we seldom slow down enough to listen or to think about what we are hearing.

It's a challenge nearly all of us face in our daily lives. The crush, the rush, the bustle, and the busy. The never-ending pressure to do more, be more, and have more. In our fast paced society, there are limitless opportunities to fill our life and our time.

Joseph Conrad said, *"Action is consolatory. It is the enemy of thought and the friend of flattering illusions."* Or, to put it another way, we can't be thinking and listening deeply if we are constantly focused on activity or speaking ourselves.

Try it sometime. Set some time aside each day and listen - really listen - to your spouse, your child, or your co-worker. You will find they will share more when you are receptive to hearing what they have to say.

CHAPTER SIX
THE EARLY BIRD
GETS THE INFLUENCE

"What we are communicates far more eloquently than anything we say or do."

~Stephen R. Covey

I attended a women's Bible study earlier this year with about 20 other women. We listened to a lesson as a group for about 30 minutes and then broke into smaller groups of five. I didn't know anyone else in my small group, but everyone else apparently knew each other already.

As we sat in a small circle, I realized it was a little awkward since no one knew who I was, the only stranger in the group. Everyone else was catching up with one another. I sat quietly, not talking at all, just listening at first.

I waited for the first opportunity and made eye contact with one of the ladies. I smiled and introduced myself which immediately broke the ice. We had a round of introductions and then enjoyed our discussion time together.

This hasn't always been the case, but it's become a habit for me now to introduce myself to someone immediately when I realize I don't know them. I used to be very quiet and withdrawn. I would never have taken the initiative to meet someone. I would have sat there and prayed no one would talk to me because I wouldn't know how I should respond.

I realize now how much quicker I can build a relationship with someone because I'm not afraid to take the first step. For many years, I simply wasn't confident in my ability to carry on a "normal" conversation. I simply lacked the skills to be social.

Be the first person to reach out. When you speak up

first, you will form an instant connection because you make the other person feel valued. It's incredible how you can connect with someone when you don't mind taking the initiative to go first. Give it a try. Try it at the grocery store – can you greet the cashier before they greet you? At the restaurant, ask the servers name immediately.

If you are at church and someone sits next to you, introduce yourself if you don't know them. If you are in the elevator, smile and greet the person who gets in with you. If you are at a social event and someone you don't know walks up to join the conversation, introduce yourself and welcome them.

Don't be afraid to be the first to speak, smile, and form an instant connection. Building a connection by reaching out first will automatically increase your influence with that person. If you truly care about them, it will be easy to show that you care.

I attended a training class recently, and I was one of the first people to arrive. Two more ladies arrived just minutes after I did, so I introduced myself to them when they walked in. We chatted for a minute before finding our places, and then someone else arrived.

I immediately introduced myself to the new arrival, but I also took it one step further. I took her over to meet the ladies I had met already and introduced them all to each other by name. As new people arrived, I would do the same each time, introduce them to someone else and learn their name.

I didn't intentionally plan it, but just making introductions increased my influence with everyone else in the room. They saw me as the "leader" of the situation simply because I took the initiative to help everyone else get comfortable.

Think about this – the first person in history to do

something makes headlines. The second person to do the very same thing is usually never mentioned.

Roger Bannister was a 25 year old man in England in 1954. He was a medical student on a track scholarship and had a talent for running fast.

He was predicted to win an Olympic Gold medal in 1952 but ended up only placing fourth. He was so disappointed he considered giving up running. Instead, he resolved to push on and break the four minute mile barrier.

It was a goal most people believed to be impossible. It was widely believed the human body simply wasn't designed to run that fast, faster than 15 miles per hour. At the time, the record stood at 4:01.

Bannister's chance came on May 6, 1954. It was cold, windy, and wet, not ideal weather for a record breaking race. He almost didn't run. At the last minute, he decided to try in spite of the weather.

Bannister wasn't the only person trying to break the record. He knew if he didn't make it, someone else could very well beat him to it.

The race probably felt like it lasted forever to Bannister, but it was over in just four short laps. His two pacers helped him run the first two laps fast, but the third lap was slower than it should have been. He had to make up the time in the final lap. He sprinted the last few hundred yards, giving everything he had to achieve the "impossible."

And, he did. He finished in 3:59.4, accomplishing what many had believed to be impossible. He made history.

His record stood for only 46 days. But, it doesn't matter – he was the first to do it, and most people don't remember the name of John Landy. He was the second person to run a mile in less than four minutes.

CHAPTER SEVEN
WINNING THE NAME GAME

"Remember that a person's name is to that person the sweetest and most important sound in any language."

~Dale Carnegie

I meet a lot of people. I meet someone new every day, and sometimes, many people in a single day. I've learned a secret. The greatest way to quickly communicate to someone you care about them is to ask for and remember their name.

I know – some of you will immediately think, "I'm not very good with names."

You won't be good at remembering someone's name until you try. You certainly won't be good at remembering someone's name if you tell yourself you can't, and therefore don't make any effort to do so. Notice you don't have any trouble remembering the names of people you meet who are important, like your new boss, or someone you are excited to meet, maybe a local celebrity.

Remembering names, especially when you meet a lot of people, is a challenge for everyone. Here are some things that help me remember names:

1) **When you meet someone, immediately repeat their name.** If someone at the Chamber Networking event introduces themselves as "Sue," then respond with "It's very nice to meet you *Sue*."

2) **Associate the name to someone else you know.** It's strange how the brain works, but it will help you remember their name if, as soon as you meet them, you think of someone else you know with that name. The brain will cognitively

recognize something that is familiar, and it will make it easier to remember their name the next time you see them. Think to yourself, "Tiffani, like my cousin Tiffani."

3) **Think of something you can associate with them and their name.** For example, if you meet someone named Sally, think of "Sally, like Sally who sold seashells by the seashore." It seems silly, but it will connect the dots allowing you to remember her name by saying it in a way that causes it to stick.

4) **Ask how they spell it.** There is almost always more than one way to spell a name. When you hear it spelled out, stop and visualize how it looks in your mind. This really helps, especially if it's a name that is not common. I often repeat it back to them. For example, when I meet someone named "Cathy," I ask if it's spelled with a "C" or a "K." She may reply, "Cathy with a C," and I repeat it back, "Nice to meet you Cathy with a C!" Note – if the person's name is very simple, like "Dan," this is probably not a great tool to use.

5) **Write it down.** It's not always possible, but in some settings this can be very helpful. For example, if I'm getting ready to teach a class and I meet someone new, I might jot their name down on my notes for quick reference when I teach the class again next week. By then, an entire week will have passed, and I will remember the person's face, but I may not remember their name. But, I will remember I wrote it down and can quickly remind myself to check if needed.

6) **Ask them to tell you something unique about themselves.** It's a great icebreaker question

anyway. "It's great to meet you Melissa. Tell me something unique about yourself." If the person isn't sure how to answer, you can follow up with "Tell me something you are passionate about." Or ask, "What's the craziest thing you've ever done?"

7) **Associate them with someone famous.** Obviously not everyone will have a name similar to someone famous. But, when it happens, it makes it easy to remember. "It's nice to meet you Teresa. Were you named after the famous Mother Teresa?"

8) **Ask how they got their name.** Maybe they don't have a name like someone famous, but asking where their name originated is a good way to connect with them. "It's a pleasure to meet you Miranda. What caused your parents to choose that name for you? Is it a family name?"

Make every effort to remember a person's name when you meet them. If you don't remember, it's best to acknowledge it, apologize, and ask again. But, if you do this, you absolutely MUST remember it from then on. Don't make them tell you a third time.

One more thing about names – get into the habit of introducing yourself to someone so that your name is easy to remember. Say it so it sticks.

I think the best example I know of is how my husband Mack introduces himself. He says, "My name is Mack, like the truck, but smaller." It never fails – people remember his name because he gives them a visual image and an emotional connection to tie it to. It may take you a little time to come up with something "sticky" about your name, but it's well worth it. My name is Ria, like Kia the car but with an "R."

CHAPTER EIGHT
IT'S NOT ABOUT YOU

"The more we elaborate our means of communication, the less we communicate."

~J. B. Priestly

Have you ever been to the doctor and been left wondering what was really wrong? Maybe he explained what was wrong with you but with a lot of acronyms or big medical words that didn't mean much to you. Then, when he left the room, you had to ask the nurse to explain it to you in real words. Or worse, you had to go home and look up what he said on the Internet. Searching Google on your smart phone at the doctor's office is a sure sign he/she communicated but didn't connect.

I once worked with a doctor who did a better job of explaining things than any other doctor I've seen. He would explain things in plain, simple words to the patient and leave out all the medical terms that most people don't know anyway. He talked *to* the patient, rather than *above* them, especially when it was a very young or very old patient. He did this so well, that it was not unusual for a patient who had been to a different doctor to ask him to "interpret" what the other doctor had said.

Particularly for those who work in very technical fields, it can be easy to talk above the "average" person because we want to demonstrate expertise. Or sometimes, we simply forget the rest of the world doesn't talk in acronyms and industry abbreviations.

Connecting is about the other person. It's not about you. You must leave your ego at the door and be willing to focus on the other person. That requires a certain level of humility in being willing to meet them on their level. It also means you are choosing to listen first or trying to understand first.

How often does this happen to you? When you are talking with someone, you spend the entire time they are talking thinking about what you are going to say. We can't wait to share a similar experience or our opinion about something. Instead of deeply listening to what they are saying, or not saying, we are completely focused on our own response.

This becomes especially important when the conversation is emotional or highly charged. When you are upset, it's easy to forget to listen first because your emotions are running high, and you *need* to share what you are thinking or feeling. If both people are focused on talking instead of listening, the conversation won't resolve anything. They will likely become even more frustrated.

When you move beyond communication and begin connecting, it's no longer about you. It's about being willing to focus on the other person first. As Epictetus once said, *"We have two ears and one mouth so that we can listen twice as much as we speak."*

Unfortunately, many people do the opposite. They talk twice as much as they listen.

Sometimes, we are so focused on delivering our message, that we neglect to focus on the other person. Have you ever asked someone how they were doing, but you didn't really listen to the answer because you were thinking of how your day was going instead?

When you ask someone a question, stop and truly listen for the answer. Intently focus on the words they say in response, how they say it, and what they don't say. Sometimes, meaning is communicated more in what isn't said.

At an old job, I answered my office phone. It was my boss. She rarely called me. She usually sent an email instead because we both were often in meetings. When she did call, it was usually urgent or very important.

That time, when I answered, I didn't answer with my usual very enthusiastic phone greeting because I had something weighing on my mind very heavy. It was a personal situation, and I was trying very hard not to bring it to work with me, but I was still emotionally down and simply not my usual cheerful self. When I answered, she immediately sensed my emotional state.

"Hey, how are you?" She asked.

"I'm fine." I replied, not fine at all.

"Are you sure? It seems like something is wrong…" She didn't probe, but she gave me the space to share if I wanted to.

"Thank you – no, I'm really okay just dealing with something. Thank you for asking."

I didn't really want to talk about it, but the fact she cared enough to drop her agenda for the call meant everything to me. She gave me the emotional room I needed, acknowledged my feelings, and treated me like my personal feelings were much more important than the work we were dealing with.

I don't remember what she really needed, and I'm sure it was important. But, I won't ever forget how much better I felt simply because she was willing to drop work and talk with me.

Be willing to drop your agenda and focus on the other person when necessary. It's important to be people oriented and to remember someone's feelings are far more important than checking off a task on your to-do list.

It's something I still work on every day.

CHAPTER NINE
I'M LIKE YOU,
IT'S OKAY TO LIKE ME

"Communication leads to community, that is, to understanding, intimacy and mutual valuing."

~Rollo May

Establishing common ground, or building rapport, with someone is often promoted as the best way to connect with someone. That may be true, but exactly what that means and how you go about it is very seldom actually mentioned.

I've attended a lot of seminars and heard many lessons on communication. Many of those lessons focus on how to establish common ground and rapport with someone. I've heard an incredible spectrum of "secrets" to building rapport, from mirroring body language to subconsciously communicating "I'm like you, so it's okay to like me."

None of that is bad, but I think it often focuses on the things to *do* instead of how to *be*. There's a huge difference. We should shift from trying to connect with someone, so they will like us, to trying to connect with someone because we care about them.

In his book, *Everyone Communicates, Few Connect*, John C. Maxwell shares three questions everyone is consciously or unconsciously asking when they meet you: *"Do you care for me? Can you help me? Can I trust you?"*

If the answer to just one of those questions is no or if the person feels like the answer is no, it will be very difficult to form a connection and communicate effectively. It's much like trying to get electricity to flow through a power cord – if the cord isn't plugged in or isn't plugged in completely, the electricity either won't flow or won't flow through well. *People won't always remember the words you use, what you say, or what you do, but they will always remember how you make them feel.*

When you first meet someone, the first step in establishing common ground is building trust in the relationship. You start building trust or creating distrust immediately when you meet someone, interact with them, or are simply around them.

In order to build trust, you must demonstrate integrity, credibility, and consistency in your words and actions. Your words and actions should be in alignment with what you tell others your values are.

For example, if you have lunch with someone and they are rude to the waiter or waitress, it will tell you everything you need to know about their character. We are all nice to the people we need something from. But, how we treat those people who can do nothing for us demonstrates whether we truly have a heart that values people.

Beyond being consistent and caring, the next step in building the relationship is establishing common ground. Take the time to learn about the other person and demonstrate your interest in them. If nothing else, you will have established common ground because you're interested in the other person. And, they're interested in themselves too.

Sometimes, it's easy to find common ground through a mutual friend or shared experience. Sometimes, it's not easy, and you must ask more about the other person to learn more. Then, listen to the answers. If you still struggle to find common ground, connect by talking about something current or global that interests almost everyone.

Barriers to finding common ground include a lack of humility, a lack of caring, a lack of respect, or a lack of understanding.

Don't assume anything when you are connecting with

other people. Each of us carries a different perspective of the world – we see the world as we are, not as it is. Because we all have different experiences in life, we will see situations differently. Terry Felber says, *"If you can learn to pinpoint how those around you experience the world, and really try to experience the same world they do, you'll be amazed at how effective your communication will become."*

Once you have listened and established some common ground, share something relevant about yourself from your experience, relationships, successes, ability, or insights that demonstrate who you are as a person. We'll get into the dialogue a little more in the next chapter.

Here are three keys to building rapport:

1) **Establish common ground or mutual experience.** This requires asking key questions (covered in depth in the next chapter) and listening to the answers. Make sure to fully listen to the answers before moving on.

2) **Don't make assumptions about the other person.** We all tend to make assumptions, but those assumptions often don't serve us well. We make snap judgments about someone based on how they dress, what they drive, how they talk, or even what they look like. Be careful to base your opinions of someone on their character, actions, and values, instead of superficial appearance.

3) **Share interesting or relevant facts about you as a person.** The key here is "interesting or relevant." Make sure the time, situation, and place are appropriate for what you want to share and be careful not to monopolize the conversation by talking about yourself.

CHAPTER TEN
RIGHT QUESTIONS,
RIGHT ANSWERS

"I remind myself every morning: Nothing I say this day will teach me anything. So if I'm going to learn, I must do it by listening."
~Larry King

Questions are an incredible tool for establishing a connection with another person. You never run out of conversation when you know how to ask questions effectively. Questions allow you to learn more about the other person: who they are, what they know, what they have experienced, how they see the world, what they feel, what they like, what they don't like, what they have learned, and what they know that you need to know.

Questions are more than just a good tool for establishing common ground and building rapport or connection. They are also one of the most powerful and effective tools for learning, leading, and influencing someone. The right questions are thought-provoking and open up dialogue, enhance communication, and allow mutual understanding.

In short, asking the right question(s) is the most effective communication tool you will ever have.

If asking questions doesn't come easily for you to start with, make a list of four or five "go to" questions you can ask in almost any situation. An example of an easy question to ask is to ask about the other person's family or children. But, make sure to ask open-ended questions. Open-ended questions are questions that require an answer other than "yes" or "no." Open-ended questions allow the other person to share as much or as little as they want, without feeling uncomfortable. They also keep the conversation going longer as you will certainly learn more with an open question.

Here are some examples of questions and how to use them in different situations:

1) **At work.** Questions asked at work allow more thorough communication and thought provoking responses. The key here is asking the question in the right way, and often, asking a follow-up question. When you are working to develop someone, answer a question with a question. It takes longer, but the rewards are huge in terms of being able to delegate responsibility and to develop and grow your team. Ask for recommendations and solutions. Ask how they propose to do something. Ask why or why not. Ask what the barriers are. Ask what the pitfalls might be. Ask what the opportunities are. Ask what else you need to know or consider. And, **listen to the answers.**

2) **At home.** With family, it's important not to ask questions that make others feel like you are probing or prying. Particularly when you know the other person is upset, make sure to ask questions gently. For example, if you ask "What's wrong?" it might feel like you are prying. It certainly comes across as aggressive or intrusive. It's more likely to shut down the other person because they don't feel safe. Instead, saying "You seem to be upset?" with a question in your voice, opens the door for them to respond with as much or as little information as they want. It's acknowledging them and giving them the emotional space to breathe and share if they want to.

3) **In a social setting.** Whether it's dinner conversation or meeting someone at a reception, a great way to break the ice is to ask them to tell you about themselves. Some people need no encouragement to talk, but being prepared with a few questions can keep the conversation going. Ask a question for the group about current affairs or what they think about so-and-so. Note: Religion and politics can be controversial, so you may want to avoid those areas.

4) **Meeting strangers.** Ask them to tell you a little about their story or about them. For example, you might be trying to establish a connection and ask someone you just met if they have children. The answer might be "yes" and they will proceed to share all about them. Or, the answer might be "no." Perhaps they wanted children and couldn't have them, or perhaps they lost a child. Not only does the conversation die right there, but you have also left them feeling uncomfortable or upset. Instead of asking if they have children, ask them to tell you about their family. Or, just ask them to tell you something about themselves. That way, they can share as much or as little as they want, and you may learn something unique, fun, or inspiring. Be prepared with a follow-up question, such as what they like about their job or what's the biggest challenge they are facing at the moment.

CHAPTER ELEVEN
CONFIDENT, NOT COCKY

"When you stop caring what people think, you lose your capacity for connection."

~Brené Brown

Without a doubt, one of the biggest barriers to connecting with other people is arrogance. If you come across as arrogant or cocky, others will quickly lose interest in connecting with you. In the words of my favorite leadership expert Mack Story, *"There's a fine line between arrogance and confidence. It's called humility."*

The difference between confidence and arrogance is something difficult to define or explain to someone, but we all know it when we see it and feel it.

When I think of someone who is arrogant, I think of someone who is self-centered.

Someone who is self-centered is constantly thinking about themselves. If you share a story with them, they have to come up with one better. It's always about them.

"You went to the beach this weekend? That's nice. I went on a five star cruise to the Bahamas."

Someone who is self-centered is always trying to put themselves in the center of attention, interrupting you, or always answering a question even if they aren't sure of the answer. They want to be seen as the "Be all, end all" and aren't happy when someone else is in the spotlight.

There are two reasons a person may be self-centered:

1) **They have a false belief and truly think they are better than everyone else.** If someone believes they are better than others, they are simply wrong. Regardless of how much money we make, how many degrees we have, what kind of house we live in, or what kind of car we drive, we are all

human just like everyone else. We all make mistakes. We all do or say things wrong sometimes, even to the people we love. We all wish we could do some things over in life. None of us are perfect. If we judge others for their mistakes, we are often overlooking our own. Pretending to know it all or have it all doesn't bring happiness in life and will cause us to feel empty as we try to pretend we are something we aren't. Life will be far easier, better, and happier if we realize our mistakes are like everyone else's failings, and we certainly all have our share.

2) **They are insecure about themselves and are trying to compensate for it.** It's okay to not have all the answers at times. It's okay to admit we don't know something. It's okay to not be perfect. So often, we feel pressured to live up to an ideal or a standard that exists only in our head. In truth, it's only when we are courageous enough to be vulnerable that we find the strength and self-confidence we have been searching for all along.

The important distinction is that confidence is good – but too much or too little is bad. Too little confidence leads to insecurity. Too much confidence may lead to arrogance.

There was a time in my life when I struggled with both of these. I shared one of these experiences in my first book, *A.C.H.I.E.V.E: 7 Keys to Unlock Success, Significance, and Your Potential.*

In 2007, I was working in a doctor's office when the office manager was terminated. I was interviewed for the position, selected, and I felt they owed it to me.

Humility wasn't something I had much of at that time. I thought I was capable of doing a better job than anyone else. I had stepped up to a leadership role in the interim. But, I had a fundamental problem - I was too proud. I wanted to control everything that went on. I wanted everything to come through me because I thought I was the only one who could and should make decisions in the office.

One morning, we were getting ready to open the office, and one of the older ladies who worked there sat down with me. What she told me changed my life. She said, "Ria, you are very capable. But, everyone is concerned because you want to control us. You act like you know everything – you don't."

She was taking a risk by sharing that with me – I was her new boss. She didn't say it specifically, but she was telling me I didn't have humility. I knew in my heart, she was right. Looking back, I am not proud of how I acted in those days. I am proud of how I responded to what she said. Rather than continue to demonstrate too much ego and pride, I heard what came out of her mouth, but I felt what came out of her heart.

It was a defining moment for me. Instead of getting mad, I actually embraced what she said. It took time, but I changed my behavior and my feelings. More importantly, I learned I didn't know everything after all. In fact, the more I learned, the more I realized what I didn't know. John Wooden said, *"It's what we learn after we know it all that counts."*

CHAPTER TWELVE
TRANSPARENT TRUTHS

"The great enemy of the truth is very often not the lie, deliberate, contrived and dishonest, but the myth, persistent, persuasive and unrealistic."

~John F. Kennedy

Transparency is something that is critical in effective communication. Transparency, honesty, and integrity affect every relationship in your life. Thomas Jefferson said, *"Honesty is the first chapter in the book of wisdom."*

We all know it's important to be honest. It's a biblical principle and one of the Ten Commandments, *"Thou shalt not lie."*

I would hope by this point in your life, you are honest. If not, I doubt my words in this short chapter will inspire you to change. It's a choice – we should choose a life of integrity. Not everyone lives with honesty and integrity in their life, their words, and their actions. It's not because they don't know it's wrong – they simply have chosen not to care.

But, there is a difference between transparency and honesty. Honesty is telling the truth, even when it might be painful. Transparency makes us vulnerable. Transparency is being real when it's not required.

As a rule, we are not very transparent in our (U.S.) society today. If someone asks how you are doing at work, regardless of how you really are, you will probably answer, "Fine. How are you?" There is almost a stigma associated with not being "fine."

We put on a mask for the outside world. A mask that hides our flaws, perceived and real. And yet, when someone is transparent and *real*, we are drawn to them. When someone is vulnerable enough to be transparent with their weaknesses, their fears, and the shadows of their inner self, we find it incredibly refreshing. That's one reason Brené Brown's work is so powerful. It's real. It's authentic. You can feel it. The greatest communicators have learned the strength behind being transparent. Sometimes, that means saying "No, I'm not okay." when someone asks.

Feeling out of alignment in life is similar to the tires on your car being out of alignment. You can still drive down the road, but there is a constant tension, or pulling, as the tires try to take you in one direction while you are trying to steer the car in another. When your life is out of alignment, your heart will pull you in one direction while you try to steer your mind in another.

I remember a time when I was faced with a decision to be transparent because my life was out of alignment.

I had been working at a hospital for several years. I loved my job. I loved the people I worked with. I loved my boss. But, I was experiencing an awakening of my purpose and passion in life and was discovering that working at the hospital was not aligned with either.

My heart was pulling me in one direction – pursue a dream – while my head was trying to steer me in another direction – stay the course. I knew I was out of alignment, and I knew why. I also knew continuing to pretend everything was great at work was not being transparent. I felt like I was deceiving those around me by pretending I was perfectly happy in my job. I also knew I had been fortunate to have the opportunities for development in the organization, and I felt like I would be letting my boss down if I resigned.

After a few months of internal tension, I realized the only thing I could do to relieve the pressure was to be transparent with my boss. Although I was uncomfortable, I shared the tension I was feeling between my heart and my head. I wanted her to know I was very grateful for the opportunities I had been given, but I also wanted her to know of my inner conflict. I knew it could potentially hurt my career path if I chose to stay. But, I also knew transparency was more important. She needed to know I might be considering another path in life and should make her decisions accordingly.

She was very supportive, and I was relieved of the tension. My heart was still pulling in one direction, but my head was no longer trying to steer me in another. As long as I was transparent, I was in alignment.

She and I agreed not to worry about it unless, and until, we needed to.

I was up front about my feelings, but I was also 100% committed to giving my best to the department and organization. Many months later, when I realized I could no longer give 100% percent, I resigned and worked out a four month notice.

Regardless of the audience, relationship, or what you are trying to communicate, transparency will increase your connection. It builds trust at a very high level. If it doesn't, you probably don't need that connection.

Transparency is the highest form of truth telling. As Mack says, *"Transparency is telling the truth when you don't have to simply because you want to."*

There is a time, place, and a way to be transparent. There are some times or situations where complete transparency would be better served in a one-on-one conversation, such as when you are offering "tough love," correcting someone, or sharing something deeply personal. Be transparent. Be truthful. But, be sensitive while doing so. Timing is critical.

Transparency isn't always comfortable. But, it's always courageous.

CHAPTER THIRTEEN
WHEN TO SAY NOTHING AT ALL

"Body language is a very powerful tool. We had body language before we had speech, and apparently, 80% of what you understand in a conversation is read through the body, not the words."

~Deborah Bull

The words we speak account for only 7% of what we are communicating. Body language, tone of voice, eye contact, facial expressions, and actions make up more than 90% of what we are communicating.

Babies aren't born with the ability to talk. However, long before they are able to form complete sentences, they are surprisingly adept at communicating their wants, likes, and dislikes to everyone around them. And, the adults around them are surprisingly responsive, demonstrating the influence the child has over them even before he/she can talk.

Simply observing a toddler will give you insight into how the child is feeling. You will be able to tell if they are happy, mad, sad, or in pain.

My cousin has a nine month old little boy. She recently brought him to visit our grandparents. My grandfather got out his guitar to sing some of the songs we loved having him sing to us when we were little. As soon as he started playing and singing, my little second cousin went crawling enthusiastically over to his Great Grandfather when he heard the music. He pulled himself up on my Grandfather's leg, so he could touch the guitar. Then, he started bouncing with the music. He couldn't talk yet, however it only took one look at him to see he was loving it.

We don't lose the ability to communicate non-verbally as we grow up. We simply don't always consciously focus on reading the non-verbal communication when interacting with others.

When we do focus, we are able to consciously "read" someone's body language even from a distance. A spouse can tell his or her partner's mood as soon as they walk in the door. A parent can tell when something is bothering their child, even if the child refuses to talk about it. Your best friend will always know when you are "down."

I love sitting in airports because they are a great place to "people watch." I don't mean staring at people in a creepy way, but taking time to observe what your fellow travelers are doing and how they are feeling. Bored, tired, sleepy, excited, frustrated, happy, sad, or mad, you can read most emotions simply through body language.

Watch a couple eating dinner in a restaurant. Pay attention, and you will find you can tell if they have a great relationship or if they are upset with one another based on their body language.

A movement analyst would tell you people, and even some animals, are sensitive to consistency in verbal and non-verbal communication. A dog, for example, is able to read visual cues when it's time to go for a walk. Words aren't needed.

The greatest communicators match their body language to what they are saying. Make sure you are communicating a consistent message. It's not only what you say. It's how you say it that makes the biggest impression.

Your body language can communicate confidence or insecurity. Amy Cuddy, a social psychologist, has done extensive research on how body language can change other people's perceptions of us and even our own body chemistry. In her TEDx talk *"Your body language shapes who you are,"* Amy talks about how standing confidently can lead to other people seeing you as more confident and also you *feeling* more confident. Your posture can affect the hormone levels in your body and cause you to feel more powerful.

If the message you are trying to communicate is very sensitive or very emotional, then how you deliver the message becomes even more important. Peter Guber said, *"Language is a more recent technology. Your body language, your eyes, your energy will come through to your audience before you even start speaking."*

If you are speaking in front of a crowd, make sure you stand tall and straight. This projects an air of self-confidence. *Be* on purpose.

If you are in an intense dialogue with someone, lean in to communicate interest. If you are having a conversation with someone in your office, turn away from your desk and face them with your entire body to signal they have your full attention.

We aren't always conscious of the message we communicate with our body language, but we should be.

Even more important than what we say or how we say it is *what we do*. Our *actions* communicate far more than words ever will because actions demonstrate who we really are. If we tell someone we are sorry, but repeat the mistake, our actions are communicating to him or her we are not truly sorry. If we tell someone we care about them, but our actions communicate a different truth, they will believe what they see instead of what they hear.

If we tell someone they are important to us, but we are late every time we meet with them, our actions are communicating they aren't really important after all.

Your actions speak the truth about your feelings, values, thoughts, and emotions. Someone can simply look at your actions to see what's truly important to you.

Actions speak louder than words ever will.

CHAPTER FOURTEEN
IT'S NOT WHAT YOU SAY, IT'S HOW YOU SAY IT

"It's never what you say, but how you make it sound sincere."
~Marya Mannes

One of the things I struggled with, and still do to a lesser degree, is having a naturally quiet voice. I don't speak loudly by nature and often come across as very soft-spoken. In the past, I didn't project my voice very well.

This could be a problem in a lot of situations. Ordering food at the drive through, conversations in a crowded restaurant, introducing myself at a noisy reception, or even having a conversation with someone who is somewhat hearing impaired were always challenges for me. I would often find myself having to repeat what I said, and I came across as very insecure. I didn't lack confidence, I simply didn't know how to communicate confidence with my voice.

Years ago, when I started teaching group fitness, I went to a training class to begin my certification process. The three day initial training was dedicated to learning the techniques, choreography, and coaching skills needed to deliver a safe, effective, and fun group fitness class.

One of the concepts we covered was using our "five voices" and what each "voice" communicated. For example, they talked about using an *intense* voice to communicate effort and a *big* voice to communicate excitement and energy. Or, using a *soft* voice to dial down the energy during some easy portions of the class.

I loved the concept because it was a great way to describe how we can change the speed, pitch, and tone of our voices to communicate differently, even if the words are the same. We actually had to practice saying a phrase using different voices, so we could hear and experience the difference.

Most people do this naturally to some degree, communicating excitement, urgency, humor, sadness or other emotions by varying the speed and tone of their voice. This is the same concept I now use when speaking from the stage or even in conversation. I became much more intentional about it once I realized there was a way to use those tools in dialogue.

Once I realized I could intentionally put a different or louder inflection in my voice, it only took a little practice before I mastered it. Sometimes, I would try to be "louder" and simply ended up yelling, which caused me to sacrifice all voice inflection for volume.

I practiced using my different voices out loud. It felt silly at first. Find a big, preferably empty, room and stand at the front of it. Then, start talking to the back wall. Have a conversation out loud and picture your voice carrying all the way to the back. It won't be easy at first, but work on speaking all the way from your belly.

Perhaps, your issue is speaking too loudly at times. If that is the case, practice having a conversation with the wall by standing right in front of it. Picture the times when you need to bring your voice down and practice that.

Find somewhere private to practice your different voices out loud or wait until you are home alone.

It's amazing how much we actually can communicate by changing our voice. It's not what we say, as much as how we say it. Klaus Schulze said, *"The human voice is the first and most natural musical instrument, also the most emotional."*

Have you ever been in the house when your kids are outside playing and one of them runs in yelling for you? Parents know instantly the urgency of the situation based on one syllable, "Mom!" So much is communicated by the tone and volume of our voice.

When we are trying to communicate to others, we can use our voice very effectively if we intentionally consider *how* we are saying what we are saying.

If you are offering an apology to someone and offer it very flippantly or carelessly, it will come across as insincere.

If you are giving a presentation at work but you use a tentative tone of voice, it will come across as though you aren't confident in the material or yourself. It won't sound credible or believable.

If you are meeting someone for the first time but your greeting is filled with anger, they won't be pleased to meet you.

If you are speaking to your spouse with short words or responses, they will think you are upset with them. Perhaps you are, but you won't resolve anything if you hurt their feelings by snapping at them.

Sometimes, we say too much, and the power of our message gets lost or diluted. When we have less time to speak, it's very important to deliver a short and effective message using the right words and tone of voice. It's not just what we say, but how we say it that determines how our message is received.

If you are a speaker or if you do any public speaking, learning how and when to use your voice effectively is one of the best tools in communicating and connecting with your audience. Spend some time thinking about what you are saying and how you can say it differently to be more effective. Don't forget there's power in saying nothing at times. Les Brown says, *"The best speakers make the fewest words go the farthest."*

CHAPTER FIFTEEN
YOUR FACE SAYS IT ALL

"You're always communicating, even when you're not talking - with your body language, your facial expressions, your eyes."
~Orlando Bloom

Facial expressions are critical components in the communication process. Often, our face says volumes without us haven spoken a single word.

Try listening more with your eyes and see how you can pick up non-verbal communication from someone's expressions. You will likely be able to read whether someone is happy, sad, or mad by their expressions. Often, you can feel the moment someone's attention shifts from you because their expressions may change when they look at something else.

Various sources report there are 42 or 43 muscles in the human face. The face can be incredibly expressive. When we add in the eyes, the face often communicates more when we're *saying* nothing at all.

I was standing in line at the grocery store not too long ago and in front of me was a mother with two young children. A little boy, about four, was eagerly checking out the candy selection while his younger sister sat in the cart. The little girl was shy, as some young children are.

She would peek at me and then look away the moment she had my attention. Then, she would turn back to face me to see if I was watching her. I couldn't help but smile at her antics as she played this peekaboo game for a few minutes.

She worked up enough courage to finally smile back, and then almost instantly, her shyness disappeared completely.

Even young children are able to read your facial expressions. We learn at an early age that a smile is a universal connection, and it's amazing how much more children will smile than adults. William Arthur Ward said, *"A smile is the universal language of kindness."*

Smile pleasantly when meeting someone and in regular conversation. This will communicate positive emotions and strengthen your connection. In the words of my mentor, motivational speaker Les Brown, *"Your smile will give you a positive countenance that will make people feel comfortable around you."*

What's interesting is how a smile can communicate even to someone who can't see you. Try this next time the phone rings. Pause for a moment before answering. Sit up straight, take a deep breath, and make sure you are smiling when you greet the caller. It sets an incredibly positive tone for your phone conversation, even though the caller can't see you. They will "hear" your smile.

Eye contact is an important part of facial communication as well. There needs to be a balance of making eye contact and looking away, especially in one-on-one conversation. If someone never looks you in the eyes, you likely won't trust them. If someone stares non-stop at you, you're likely to feel uncomfortable.

I read that Dale Carnegie suggested looking into someone's eyes long enough to register what color they are, and then look away. It's also important to break your gaze to the side rather than down. Looking down can come across as submissive or low self-esteem.

Consistent eye contact indicates attention, especially when talking with someone. Make sure when you break contact for a brief period, you aren't glancing at your phone or computer screen. That indicates your attention is being pulled away and is really focused on something or someone else.

One of my previous bosses demonstrated focused

attention really well. When I went in to her office for a meeting, she would roll her chair around, so we didn't have a desk between us. She would face me directly and give me her complete attention by looking at me while we talked.

She set the example of giving me her complete attention, and she expected mine. She wouldn't break off to check her email or sneak a look at her phone while we talked. I felt important to her.

It's something I have tried to make sure I do all the time. If someone is talking to me, I try to face them directly and make sure I'm fully focused on them. It's certainly fine to break away for a moment, but come back to them immediately. If someone else walks up to join the conversation, look at them and smile or nod briefly, then return to the conversation. That way, you aren't telling your conversation partner someone else is more interesting.

It's not always possible of course. If I'm cooking dinner and Mack comes into the kitchen, I can't give him my full attention, or we would be eating burned dinner. If something like that happens, it's okay to say "Please excuse me while I finish this. Then, I can listen to you better." That way, you have acknowledged the other person, made them feel important, and asked permission to complete what you were doing. It will give emotional space for you both.

Conversely, if you need to break off a conversation for some reason, starting to turn your face away can indicate you need to exit. Make sure to politely explain and excuse yourself, so you don't leave the other person wondering why you left.

CHAPTER SIXTEEN
TALK WITH YOUR HANDS

"You cannot shake hands with a clenched fist."

~Indira Gandhi

When I first started speaking professionally, I realized I would benefit from professional coaching. I had been speaking on stage for years through work or teaching classes, but when I decided to pursue a speaking career, I knew I had a lot to learn.

I went through several months of coaching to improve my speaking skills, but one of the most difficult things for me to change was what I was doing with my hands when I talked. Until my speaking coach pointed it out, I never consciously thought about it. Once he mentioned it, I realized I fidgeted with my hands continuously while talking. Not just when speaking from the stage, but even in light conversation with one person.

What's interesting is now that I'm aware of what my hands are doing, I'm also far more interested in what other people do with their hands when they talk. It's always neat to watch other people who are speaking on stage with the sound muted. Then, you can really focus on their body language, especially how they use their hands.

Some people are very animated talkers with wide, sweeping hand gestures. Some people are very still and barely move at all.

I recently sat with Mack while he was on the phone with someone. We were in the car, waiting to go in to a meeting, and he needed to finish the call before we went in.

Mack is a very dynamic speaker, even on the phone. The caller couldn't see him, and yet as he talked, his energy level kept rising, and he began to use his hands more. The more energy he got, the bigger his hand gestures got. That is often the case with animated speakers. The more energy and passion they have for what they are talking about, the more expressive their hand gestures are.

The most effective speakers use their hands to communicate, but they do not overwhelm the listener or their audience. In other words, simply using your hands when you talk isn't enough. It's what you are doing with them.

Hand gestures can communicate many things. When you are angry, you might make threatening hand gestures, pointing fingers, or shaking a fist at someone. When you are upset, you might simply wrap your arms around yourself. When you are excited about crossing the finish line at a race, you might give a fist pump to signal victory. In *"Leaders Eat Last"* Simon Sinek wrote about how a handshake communicates trust in a business deal. Or, if someone refuses to shake, it communicates distrust.

Here are some thoughts on using hand gestures effectively while speaking:

1) **Stay in control**. Keep your hand gestures in a loose square box in front of you, unless you're using them to describe something that's large or distant. If you find your hands waving wildly above your head, you've gone too far and will communicate an "out of control" feeling.

2) **Be intentional, not distracting**. You don't want to simply move your hands for the sake of movement, but you do want your gestures to emphasize a point or underscore a statement. Too much movement or constant movement is distracting.

3) **Be smooth**. Jerky hand movements come across as upset or angry. Passionate but purposeful movements should be fluid.

4) **Avoid pointing at the listener or audience**. Yes, you want to emphasize your point, but doing so by pointing fingers can come across as attacking or blaming. They will feel the meaning even if you don't mean it.

5) **Be consistent**. If you are using your left hand to represent one point and the right hand to represent another, make sure you stay consistent with which side is which when talking.

6) **Be open.** Opening your arms up with palms facing upward can seem open and inviting or inclusive. Avoid a palms down or pushing away motion if you are trying to draw in the audience.

7) **Don't be afraid to be still sometimes.** Yes, using hand gestures can make you a more dynamic speaker in conversation and speaking on stage. But, don't forget about the power of stopping for a moment and simply being still to draw the audience in. Think of a singer who brings home the last note with stillness.

8) **Remember not every hand gesture has a universal meaning.** We will talk more about this in a later chapter. But remember, different cultures often communicate differently, especially with hand gestures.

If you can, try to video yourself while speaking or practicing a presentation. Watch the replay with the sound off, so you can focus on gestures.

I don't like to watch myself on video, but it's a very valuable exercise for improving my communication skills.

CHAPTER SEVENTEEN
HANDS ON, HANDS OFF

"Too often we underestimate the power of a touch, a smile, a kind word, a listening ear, an honest compliment, or the smallest act of caring, all of which have the potential to turn a life around."

~Leo Buscaglia

As humans, we are wired so that physical contact releases oxytocin into our bodies which helps us feel good, more social, and more connected. As Simon Sinek said, *"It (Oxytocin) is the reason it feels nice to hold hands with someone and the reason young children seem to always want to touch and hug their mothers...it is part of the reinforcing bond."*

There is no doubt physical contact can reinforce the bond we have with someone. I was working at a hospital many years ago when they started a "skin-to-skin" initiative for newborns and their mother. Advantages of increased skin-to-skin contact between infant and mother are well documented and include a more alert baby who sleeps better, cries less, gains weight faster, and even has better brain development.

We see many examples of adults making physical contact to increase their bond with others as well. Athletes give high-fives or bear hugs in celebration while business executives often greet one another by shaking hands. However, understanding how to appropriately use physical contact to establish or increase a bond varies widely between gender, age, and cultural background.

Physical contact is one of the murkier areas where the boundaries are not always well defined. There may be a chance of offending someone if you overstep those boundaries. You could be invading their personal space which varies from person to person.

There are many different ways to establish physical contact such as handshakes, hugs, shoulder pats, fist bumps, kisses, back slaps, and so on. Other than handshakes, most forms of physical contact are reserved for someone you know and with whom you already have a relationship. If you don't know the person, you may not intend the gesture to be offensive, but if the other person feels like you have overstepped their boundaries, it can feel inappropriate and create distrust.

If you are traveling to another country or working with someone from another culture, its best to research the cultural norms before interacting with them, if possible.

Here are some general guidelines I use related to the use of physical contact (in the U.S.) and also when to avoid it *in a professional environment*. If in doubt, err on the side of caution and allow the other person to initiate contact if they desire.

Hands On…

- **When first meeting someone, greet them by handshake, unless otherwise indicated.** A man may wait until the woman initiates the handshake. One thing I will say here is your handshake says a lot about you**. When shaking hands, firmly grip the person's hand, give a brief shake, and acknowledge them by looking into their eyes briefly.** Then, let go. It doesn't need to be very long. Avoid hand crushing, but make sure your grip is firm enough to communicate confidence.

- **When you already know someone, greet them with a handshake or hug.** There is already a precedent for your relationship and contact.

- **Greeting someone you have already made a connection with.** I hug lots of people, even if I'm just meeting them. The key here is to have already formed a connection with them and knowing that an *appropriate* hug is a great way to deepen that connection. Avoid prolonged contact – a quick side hug is usually sufficient. Men should let women take the lead initiating hugs.

Hands Off...

- **When working with a subordinate, especially of a different gender.** If you are in a position of authority over someone, you should avoid initiating physical contact other than the professional handshake unless you know them well. Then, perhaps use a friendly, professional, arm/shoulder pat. In general, a lot of physical contact at work with subordinates should be avoided.

- **When you are angry.** If you are angry or upset, your physical contact or even hand gestures (such as pointing fingers) will be harsher, rougher, and much easier to be taken as inappropriate.

- **When the person appears uncomfortable.** There are some organizations that appreciate a more "family" feeling in their culture, and you may see more hugs in general there. That's perfectly fine, as long as both parties are comfortable, and it's appropriate physical contact that doesn't violate someone's space, feelings, or emotions.

CHAPTER EIGHTEEN
YOUR STYLE

"We are all born with a unique genetic blueprint, which lays out the basic characteristics of our personality as well as our physical health and appearance...And yet, we all know that life experiences do change us."

~Joan Vinge

Each of us has a basic personality type that reflects our natural style, tendencies, and traits. Understanding your personality will simply make your communications much more effective.

It's important to know your natural tendencies, so you can overcome them. For example, if you are a naturally shy person who doesn't like to talk, you can learn to ask more questions to keep the other person talking most of the time.

Or, if you are a person who doesn't like details, remember not everyone is like you. Some people actually prefer to hear more details.

Work to discover your preferred personality traits, so you can leverage them effectively.

There is an incredible number of personality tests, surveys, or profiles you can take to help you discover your personality style. Myers-Briggs, DISC, Hogan Personality Inventory, The Animal Quiz, Keirsey Temperament Sorter, Behavioral Assessments, and many others.

I have taken a number of them over the years. Each offers a little insight and suggests how to apply that insight to complement your style as a connector and communicator. However, while we learn some of our strengths (and weaknesses) related to our personality, most of us also feel some resentment when labeled.

We like the good things that our personality profile

says, and we refute the negative things. I think to myself "Yes, I'm sensitive, but I'm not a sucker!" while reading the character traits of my DISC profile.

Personality tests aren't bad. In fact, they can be great tools to help you understand your personality and the personalities of others. But remember, one tool doesn't do every job.

Taking personality quizzes and profiles can help raise your self-awareness. Self-awareness is a sign of emotional intelligence. Daniel Goleman talks about this in his book, Emotional Intelligence. He says, *"Self-awareness – recognizing a feeling as it happens – is the keystone of emotional intelligence…Handling feelings so they are appropriate is an ability that builds on self-awareness."*

It's important to know both the strengths and weaknesses related to your basic personality traits, so you can work to improve.

Epictetus said, *"Imagine for yourself a character, a model personality, whose example you determine to follow, in private as well as in public."*

For example, if you know yourself to be more task focused, recognize that and look for situations where you need to focus on being more people-centric. A funeral is not a time to be task focused – there isn't a checklist for grief. It's a time to be more focused on the feelings and emotions of others.

On the other hand, there are other situations where it's necessary to push forward with carrying out the task, and there isn't time to really focus on sympathy.

Once you understand yourself, you can start trying to understand others. Then, apply what you know to enhance your communication style.

Mack and I have completely different personality styles naturally. In fact, early in our relationship we would joke about being so completely opposite of one another. I like vanilla – he likes chocolate. I like quiet dinners with good conversation – he likes to watch the news since we are eating and can't talk much anyway. I am a morning person – he is a night owl. I like to plan every detail of my day – he is a spur of the moment kind of guy.

While we laughed about the differences, they caused some conflicts early in our relationship. I had to learn to be more spontaneous, and he had to learn to give me an idea of what we were doing over the weekend, so I could prepare. I had to learn to communicate directly to him in quick bullet points, and he had to learn to be patient with my love of details.

Knowing your style is simply the first step in improving yourself. Maxwell Maltz said it best, *"The 'self-image' is the key to human personality and human behavior. Change the self-image and you change the personality and the behavior."*

I realize I have a natural inclination to serve and don't like to tell others "No" when asked to do something. I have, in the past, allowed myself to become overcommitted simply because I wouldn't tell someone "No, I can't help."

Recognizing that, I am now very careful to consider commitments, and I usually ask for time to think about it before committing. That way, I don't feel too much pressure in the moment. It's much easier to evaluate carefully when I'm not "on the spot." And often, I make a different decision than I would have immediately because I have time and space to think it through.

Being more aware of your natural style will help you become conscious of when it's working for you and when it isn't.

CHAPTER NINETEEN
YOUR STYLE UNDER STRESS

"The mind can go either direction under stress—toward positive or toward negative."

~Frank Herbert

Regardless of our basic personality traits, most of us act, think, and speak differently when we are experiencing stress. If you often speak without thinking, you may become even more impulsive in a stressful situation and say whatever comes to mind, offending or hurting others. Especially when stressed, be mindful of acting with intention rather than reacting with emotion.

I took the Hogan Personality Inventory many years ago. It's one of the more comprehensive personality profiles I have taken, and my report afterwards was very in depth. It covered quite a few dimensions of my personality. What I really appreciated was it included information on how each dimension of my personality would change under stress.

I sat down with the Director of Leadership Development at the organization where I worked, and she helped me understand it. She took time to be thorough, going through each dimension and what it meant. When she got to the last section, she said, "Now, let's learn about the dark side of Ria."

I said, "I don't have a dark side!"

I wasn't sure what having a dark side meant, but I was pretty sure it wasn't a good thing.

"The dark side is what we become when we are under stress. Stress tends to change how we respond in situations, and our personality can actually change when we become stressed." She explained.

Feeling better, I realized everyone had a "dark side," so I was in good company.

I conceded, "Oh, okay. Well, I suppose I do have a

dark side then."

It's not surprising that our communication style is often the first thing to change when we are feeling stressed. Our brain actually responds to the cortisol (stress hormone) our body produces by increasing our feelings of "fight or flight."

When I'm stressed, I become less communicative overall. The higher my stress level, the quieter I become. And when I do communicate, I'm much more likely to be short and snappy.

Knowing this, I try to be very conscious of my responses when I'm stressed. If I get an email that is upsetting or causes stress, I simply won't respond to it until I've had a chance to calm down. I choose not to respond until I can respond based on values instead of the emotions of the moment.

The higher our stress level, the more reactive we tend to become. When we are reactive, we are responding to a situation based on what we are feeling – our emotions. When we are more reactive than proactive, we respond emotionally to feelings of hurt, anger, or fear.

When we are proactive, we are responding to a situation based on what we truly value.

Years ago, I was waiting tables on a busy Saturday night. The kitchen was swamped, there was over an hour wait for guests to get a table, and all of us who were serving were running crazy in order to keep up.

We had been busy for a couple of hours, longer than our normal dinner rush. Because we had been so swamped, we weren't able to keep up with washing the dishes and restocking clean ones. At the soda fountain, we were running out of the clean, frozen mugs we normally provided for our customers.

Our policy stated if you used the last clean mug, you

were responsible for going to the freezer and pulling out the huge rack of clean, frozen mugs, so the next person wasn't stuck without a supply.

One of the best servers, normally a calm and competent server with a happy smile, started to get stressed out. She was feeling stretched too thin. She went to pick up an order from the kitchen and loaded up her tray with food for her table.

Almost running, she hustled toward the dining room. Then, she realized she had forgotten a requested refill. Holding the tray on her shoulder with one hand, she grabbed the last clean mug and filled it with ice and soda on her way out of the kitchen.

Someone called her back to remind her it was her responsibility to go get the rack of frozen mugs from the walk-in freezer since she used the last one.

For her that night, it was the last straw.

She slammed the tray against the kitchen wall, breaking dishes and splashing food everywhere.

"I QUIT!" She yelled out in frustration and stormed out the back door of the kitchen.

The rest of us just looked at each other. She couldn't quit – she had customers!

We managed to adjust and finished the night with no other major catastrophes. Patty (name changed) did return to work after she calmed down, and life went on. It was a good example of how someone who is under a lot of stress can and will change their normal behavior and communication style. Be aware of how stress impacts you, so you can avoid your dark side.

CHAPTER TWENTY
SPEAK NO EVIL

"I have noticed that nothing I never said ever did me any harm."
~Calvin Coolidge

Have you ever said something in the heat of the moment that you later regretted?

Odds are good that you have. We might later blame it on a short temper, or being ill, or the heat of the moment. But once it's said, it can't be taken back.

Words can become sharp and cruel weapons. They can also be used to quickly hurt others. Perhaps that's why Laurence Peter said, *"Speak when you are angry - and you'll make the best speech you'll ever regret."*

When it comes to communication and connection, not saying something can be far more powerful, and helpful, than saying something you will regret later.

Years ago, I was teaching group fitness at a local gym. There was a new instructor going through the certification process and videoing his class was part of the final "exam." I showed up to support him as I always tried to do when new instructors were getting started.

If nothing else, I could be there to turn on the video camera and set up the tripod. Since it was a 5:30am class, I knew attendance would be lighter and an extra set of hands to help would be appreciated. I didn't know Kevin (name changed) very well. I had only said hello in passing.

He videoed his class, and I stuck around for a few minutes afterward to help him get the room cleaned up. As we walked out together after the class, he turned to me and said, "I just wanted to say thanks for helping out this morning. And, I want to let you know I, and my whole church, will be praying for you and the baby."

Since I wasn't pregnant, nor planning to be, you can imagine my shock.

"Um, thanks. But, I'm not expecting." I stammered out, offended that he apparently thought I looked pregnant and now had an entire congregation praying for me.

He looked like he had swallowed a frog. Whole.

"You aren't? I mean, I'm sorry, I guess I thought…." He trailed off, apparently deciding (correctly) he was only making it worse.

"Whatever made you think that?" I asked.

"Someone told me." He confessed.

It took me a few minutes to realize he simply had mistaken me for another instructor who *was* expecting and was due in a few weeks. Feeling better about it, I explained the case of mistaken identity. Then, we shared a few laughs about it.

"I'll be more careful about what I say next time," he chuckled as we left the gym.

It doesn't always turn out to be funny like it did that time. Words spoke in anger or grief can be very hurtful and could destroy a relationship that took years to develop. Often, the people we love the most are the ones who have the most power to hurt us with their words.

In the inevitable event you say something you later regret, here are three tips for moving forward:

1) **Apologize.** Immediately. Sincerely. Thoroughly. If you said something inappropriate, hurtful, or wrong, offer a sincere apology. The key word here is "sincere." Don't apologize unless you mean it. A heartfelt apology won't fix everything, but it can go a long way toward repairing the relationship. Admit your mistake. Accept responsibility for your words and the pain they caused.

2) **Don't make excuses.** Sure, we all feel like we deserve a little extra grace when things aren't going our way, but it's important not to make an excuse when you hurt someone with your words. You chose to speak, and you chose the words that came out of your mouth. There is no excuse if you said something intentionally hurtful. Even if it was unintentional, don't make an excuse. See #1 above and apologize instead. Then, explain you didn't intend to hurt or offend. It's not an excuse to declare your intent and can help clarify your meaning.

3) **Accept the consequences.** Regardless of a sincere apology, there are some instances where you said something that caused irreparable damage. We choose our actions, words, and deeds, but we do not get to choose our consequences. That's a painful lesson, but learning it now will prevent it from happening in the future. Think before you speak next time. Even when angry, frustrated, sad, or mad, walk away if you must and return to the conversation when you are in a better emotional state.

As William Drummond stated well, *"Put a bridle on thy tongue; set a guard before thy lips, lest the words of thine own mouth destroy thy peace...on much speaking cometh repentance, but in silence is safety."*

CHAPTER TWENTY ONE
DIFFICULT DIALOGUE

"The ultimate measure of a man is not where he stands in moments of comfort and convenience, but where he stands at times of challenge and controversy."

~Martin Luther King, Jr.

I stared at the piece of paper in my hand in shock. It was a much anticipated bonus check from work. I had worked extremely hard for it all month.

Our bonus structure was simple and based off of our target sales goal for the month. The entire bonus amount was split evenly between the full-time employees, as long as they had not missed more than eight hours of work that month.

What made this month so special was we had reached the top tier sales goal, and one of the employees had resigned last month. We still had not hired a replacement, so there were only two of us in the office, meaning the bonus would be split two ways instead of three. With just two of us working, it had been an incredible effort to make our top sales goal for the month. We were both excited to receive our bonus checks.

But, when I opened the envelope, I just sat there in disbelief. It was several hundred dollars short of what I was expecting.

I couldn't believe it – we had worked so hard, and the numbers had clearly been on target for the month. Yet, I had received only a middle tier bonus check.

Starting to become upset, I rushed to my co-worker's office.

"Open your bonus check." I insisted.

"What? We reached top tier this month!" She grabbed a letter opener and slit open the envelope.

"Mine's short too!" She exclaimed in disbelief.

"What are we going to do? How could they cheat us like that?"

It was time for some difficult dialogue with my boss. It would be difficult because it would be emotional. I was upset and angry, feeling slighted. It would be difficult because it would be sensitive. Anytime you have a discussion about money with your boss, it could escalate to a sensitive topic. It was going to be difficult because we clearly had differing opinions. I thought I earned the top tier bonus, but that wasn't what I received.

I didn't believe it was a deliberate effort to cheat us, but I knew something wasn't right. I needed clarification. I didn't want to appear ungrateful. I was normally reserved about money, but I was determined to ask why we didn't get the full amount.

I marched down the hall to the boss's office with my check in hand. Right behind me was my co-worker. She was curious to see what happened.

In life, at work and at home, there will be some conversations which are more difficult to have than others. Sometimes, we know they are coming, but sometimes the need for difficult dialogue pops up unexpectedly.

Conversations where there are a lot of emotions or a lot at stake will always be more critical, and often, more difficult to have successfully. When this is the case, it's even more important to make sure you are connecting and communicating clearly, completely, and effectively.

For most of us, when the time for difficult dialogue comes, we find ourselves emotionally ill-prepared to have the conversation we need to have.

Think about what happens when the need for difficult dialogue comes around. Something happens. There's a situation you don't like. Or, you think a situation is about to happen that you won't like. Either way, you feel like you are out of control, and it's not pleasant. You have a few facts in front of you, and you immediately jump to a conclusion that helps you make sense of those facts.

In my case, it was a bonus check that was less than I expected. I immediately began to tell myself what happened. "He tried to short us from our full bonus," was running through my head as I stalked down the hall.

I had absolutely no reason to think there was an intentional effort to short me. I had been there nearly a year and had never had a paycheck or bonus check come up short. So, why did I immediately jump to that conclusion? I was trying to justify what happened in my head by making up the pieces of the story I didn't have.

I paused just before knocking on the door. I knew this conversation had three possible outcomes: 1) It was all a mistake and would be corrected; 2) It wasn't a mistake, and I would simply be told I was wrong; or 3) I could be terminated for disrespect.

I wasn't too worried about the third outcome, and I knew the difference in getting the first outcome or the second could very well depend on how I said what I planned to say when I walked in.

When it comes to difficult dialogue, it's smart to pause and consider what could happen, what you want to happen, and what you should do differently to help achieve the outcome you want.

In my case, there was simply an error. My co-worker and I both received an additional check with the difference. However, if I had appeared ungrateful, angry, or been accusatory, that may not have happened. We'll talk more in the next few chapters about situations with difficult dialogue and how to resolve them.

CHAPTER TWENTY TWO
STRAIGHT TALK
- RESOLVING CONFLICT

"Peace is not absence of conflict, it is the ability to handle conflict by peaceful means."

~Ronald Reagan

When there is a need for those tough conversations, straight talk is talking through a conflict and resolving the issue in a way that allows both sides to "win." If both sides can't get a win, then there shouldn't be a deal. Straight talk isn't always comfortable – most often, it's difficult to do because it requires us to deal with some issues that are sensitive, emotional, or painful.

The first step to straight talk is being ready to listen first. If you aren't ready to listen, you aren't ready to have difficult dialogue. I want to repeat myself because it's that important – **if you aren't ready to listen, you aren't ready to have difficult dialogue.** First, focus on the facts and seek to understand the other person's perspective.

Being able to listen first demonstrates you are able to stay in control of your emotions. Emotions can very quickly make a situation explosive. It's critical to make sure you are ready to *respond* calmly, instead of letting your emotions cause you to *react* uncontrollably. If tempers are running high, it's much easier to be offended.

Sometimes, we forget to focus on what we really want and get caught up in the need to be right or the need to be in control.

Do the following when you find yourself in a difficult dialogue situation:

- **Start by expressing what you truly want.** It seems simple. Often, by clarifying the goal of the conversation, you can help set the tone and direction for the dialogue. Be clear – contrast what you truly DON'T want with what you truly DO want. For example, "Steve, I don't want to start a fight about our project at work, but I do have some concerns about us missing a deadline and getting off track. Can we talk about it?"

- **Stay aware of your actions and emotions.** Have you ever yelled at someone because you were late for work and later felt bad about it? At times, do you change your actions because you are stressed? When the situation is a stressful or sensitive one, we often change our behavior in response to what we are feeling. Make sure to take a step back and honestly determine if your actions are out of alignment with how you know you should be acting. Then, make adjustments.

- **Don't hesitate to apologize when necessary and appropriate.** It's a simple thing, but an appropriate apology can totally turn around difficult dialogue creating a responsive environment for resolving the issue. The key is having an appropriate apology. That means it's necessary and offered sincerely. It won't fix everything, but it demonstrates your humility and a desire to correct your mistake.

- **Make sure you are communicating based on facts.** Don't assume something simply because you have a piece of the story. Give the other person the benefit of the doubt until there is no doubt.

- **Ask questions to make sure you understand correctly.** Instead of immediately being offended by a remark, ask questions to make sure it was intended as an insult. More than likely, the other person is reacting instead of responding and didn't mean to hurt you. They simply reacted without thinking about the consequences. If you confirm their intent, often there was a misunderstanding or a mistake.

- **Practice truly listening – rephrase content or paraphrase to ensure the message is clear.** Don't just listen to what the other person is saying – listen to what they aren't saying. Communication is mostly non-verbal, so don't make the mistake of focusing on the words only and miss the larger part of the message. Focus on what isn't being said and how it is being delivered to you. Communication is two way – don't forget to receive the message as well as deliver your own.

- **Mutually move forward. Together, decide what the next step is.** More on this in the next chapter.

These principles can be very helpful with difficult dialogue. Being able to use them well doesn't happen accidently. Take the time and effort to practice using them in different situations. Perhaps you want to start with a minor conflict and work up to larger issues. The more you apply these principles, the easier difficult dialogue will become.

Often, you might have good intentions to use them the next time "Difficult Dialogue" comes up, but your good intentions may fly right out the window when your emotions take over. That's why it's easier to look ahead and plan for a very specific conversation where you can use them. Always, practice, practice, and practice some more. You will still get it wrong sometimes – but learn from those mistakes and resolve to do better next time.

CHAPTER TWENTY THREE
MOVING FORWARD TOGETHER

"I define connection as the energy that exists between people when they feel seen, heard, and valued; when they can give and receive without judgment; and when they derive sustenance and strength from the relationship."

~Brené Brown

When we face difficult dialogue, we often get so wrapped up in what we want, that we forget we are only half of the equation. It's important to remember both sides need a "win." Connecting isn't about who wins or who loses – it's about both sides winning. If you can't reach a mutual agreement, or "win-win" as Stephen R. Covey called it, then there should be "no deal."

Agree to disagree if that's what must happen. Having effective, difficult dialogue should help you resolve issues. If it doesn't, then walk away. Agree mutually to disagree if you can't achieve "win-win."

Often, one person has a more dominant personality style than the other. If both aren't careful, the less dominant person will find themselves simply giving in to avoid more conflict. This may solve the short term problem, but it's likely to cause even more friction later down the road.

If you are the more dominant personality type, you must make more of an effort to be more sensitive when engaged in difficult dialogue. If you are a less dominant person, you must intentionally stand your ground at times. If something is important to you, stand firm.

Both sides should remember to keep a firm grasp on why they are having the discussion to begin with and what they want to accomplish.

For example, a couple might be in the middle of a fight about where they want to spend the holidays this year. He wants to spend Christmas Day at his mother's house, and she wants to spend Christmas Day at her mother's house.

It appears they want different things. If we take a step back, we can see they both want the same thing – a special Christmas celebration with family. There may be several possible solutions to the scenario. All they must do is find the one that is a win-win. They should find the common ground and work from there by considering the possibilities that would satisfy both.

One solution might be to split up for a few hours on Christmas Day. She can go to her mother's house, and he can go to his mother's house. Or, they might decide to rotate each year – this year at one house and next year at the other house. Or, perhaps they decide Christmas Eve would be a good time to visit one and on Christmas Day they could visit the other.

When we commit to finding a solution that works for both sides, we can brainstorm around *how* to make it happen, instead of spending our energy blaming the other person because it won't work out. In the words of Wayne Dyer, *"Conflict cannot survive without your participation."*

Resolving conflict is about respecting the differences of others and valuing the strength of working together.

Here are four things to remember when moving forward:

1) **Create a safe environment.** When it comes to having difficult dialogue and resolving a conflict, it helps to have the conversation in a "safe" place or somewhere neutral. Make sure the other person doesn't feel attacked or threatened before you begin the conversation. This might mean going to them in their office or choosing a quiet spot where you can

talk alone. Either way, start out by creating a safe environment.

2) **Take action.** Often, at the end of difficult dialogue, regardless of outcome, you are emotionally drained. You are simply ready to be done with the conversation. Don't forget to make sure you are ready to move forward and actually set some action steps as needed. **Make sure everyone involved is clear on how to move forward.** Accountability and following up on action items are great ways to build trust into the relationship. If you are in doubt about what the action items are, summarize them as you wrap up the conversation or meeting.

3) **Agree to disagree, if needed.** Discuss this option at the start. If it's simply impossible to come to a mutual agreement, agree to disagree and walk away. Keeping your relationship intact is far more important than "winning" the argument.

4) **Work on yourself.** Sooner or later, you will be in difficult dialogue, and you will realize while you are diligently applying the difficult dialogue principles and working to resolve the issue, the other person isn't. They may be more interested in being right or winning at your expense. You can't fix them. You can only work on yourself. It's up to you to demonstrate a good example and influence them in a positive way. Hitting them on the head with a book on communication is probably not going to convince them it's worth reading.

CHAPTER TWENTY FOUR
SOCIAL SITUATIONS

"Shyness is about the fear of social judgments - at a job interview or a party you might be excessively worried about what people think of you. Whereas an introvert might not feel any of those things at all, they simply have the preference to be in a quieter setting."

~Susan Cain

I'm not shy. Nor would I consider myself an introvert. But, I certainly have a preference for a quieter setting. I always have. Not because I'm shy or introverted, but because I didn't always know how to connect with others.

I didn't like being in a social setting where I might be expected to have a conversation, because I was afraid I might say the wrong thing. Or worse, I wouldn't be able to think of anything to say. I didn't need to worry if I avoided social situations.

I simply thought I didn't have good communication skills, and there wasn't much I could do about it. I thought the ability to have an interesting conversation with someone was a skill you were either born with or without.

So, I didn't really try for a long time. It was easier to tell myself I wasn't very good at it. If Mack was around, I let him do most of the talking. That worked well because Mack naturally talks more than I do. He's got more to say.

However, I realized there would be times in life when I need those communication or conversation skills, and I wouldn't have them. In 2013, I realized I needed to get very intentional about improving my social setting communication skills.

I was in Guatemala with John C. Maxwell for an international training event. I was asked to give an interview for a short video they were creating about the event and those of us doing the training. They intended to use it to raise awareness. On the third day of our trip, they called me to come down to the pool for the interview.

Mack stayed in the hotel room, and I walked down the hall to the elevator. Much to my surprise, when I turned the corner, I ran into John waiting on the elevator!

It took me a few seconds to absorb that he was dressed to go to the pool – bathing suit and all. I awkwardly realized I had absolutely nothing to say. At the time, I didn't like unexpected or unplanned social situations of any kind because I always felt unprepared.

Mack and I had made a short video with John a few days earlier, but I didn't think he would remember me. There were 150 of us on the training team. Plus, he meets thousands of people every week.

We got onto the elevator, and he pushed the button for the ground level. I just nodded silently.

This was the chance of a lifetime – a few minutes to ask the greatest leadership guru in the world a question, and I had absolutely nothing to say. I was tongue tied.

Fortunately, he wasn't. Either remembering me or spotting my ID badge, he knew I was part of the training team. "Tell me about your training today. Did you get to go out to a site?" He asked me excitedly. He was leading the initiative to train 20,000 Guatemalan leaders on leadership principles that week. That's why we were all there.

I was saved! That was a question I could answer, so I started talking. It was a memorable experience for two reasons. One, it's probably the only time I will ever have a chance to say I rode down the elevator with John C. Maxwell while he was wearing a T-shirt and swimming trunks. And two, it helped me realize I needed to learn how to talk to people more effectively.

I will never be "naturally gifted" like some people are, but I've certainly improved tremendously. I no longer fear an unexpected or unplanned opportunity to talk to someone. Here are some tips that help me connect in social situations:

1) **Ask questions.** It seems simple, but for a while, I had a list of questions prepared to use in almost any social setting to get the conversational ball rolling. Make yourself a short list of 3-5 key questions that work for you. "How" questions or "What" questions work very well.

2) **Share one interesting thing about yourself.** If for some reason your question falls flat, be prepared to share an interesting story about yourself. For example, I might share my John Maxwell elevator story to get people laughing with me. It's self-deprecating, which works well at connecting with people because it shows humility. It also says I don't take myself too seriously.

3) **Ask for their opinion on something current**. Don't ask who they plan to vote for. Ask for their thoughts and their perspective, "How do you think the election will affect our economy next year?" Or, "What impact do you think the Olympics will have on the host city?"

4) **Ask why.** When someone shares an opinion, decision, or thought, ask why. 99% of the time it will lead to an entire conversation.

CHAPTER TWENTY FIVE
CONNECTING WITH A CROWD

"There are always three speeches, for every one you actually gave. The one you practiced, the one you gave, and the one you wish you gave."

~Dale Carnegie

I'm often asked if I get nervous when I speak. The answer is no. Perhaps because I've done it so many times, but I really can't ever remember getting nervous before speaking. I've spent over 12,000 hours on stage, as a speaker and group fitness instructor. I've learned the key to confidence is being prepared and that's even more true when it comes to communicating from the stage and connecting to a crowd.

Preparation for both content and delivery is critical to fighting off stage fright and anxiety. The more prepared you are, the better you will be able to handle unexpected problems big and small. A prepared speaker will be able to adjust as needed to a different room, stage layout, an interruption, or even a longer or shorter time slot. They won't whine. They will shine.

Practice will enhance your delivery skills. Sometimes, it helps to start practicing when no one else is home. Then, when you feel a little more comfortable, recruit someone to watch or record yourself if possible. Then, go back and watch yourself. I really dislike doing this, but it's incredibly helpful. Practice your jokes while talking casually to other people, that way you know what works and what doesn't.

I think it's important to say that while practice is a huge help in feeling comfortable, the best speakers don't memorize an entire speech word for word. They remember some key stories, vignettes, or maybe have an outline prepared. If you try to remember your entire speech word for word, and then forget something, you won't be able to recover. Also, a completely memorized speech can come across as very robotic as you focus on delivering the words exactly as planned.

My most memorable example of how preparation helped me stay focused happened years ago. I was teaching on stage with someone when we realized a lady in the class was apparently unstable. She was upset about something and took her frustrations out on the person I was teaching with, first by yelling. Then, she started throwing objects at the stage! I took over the class and continued to teach while my partner tried to deal with the situation quietly. She had to call the police to forcefully remove the troubled lady from the facility, all while I delivered the planned program.

That's an extreme example, but there is absolutely no way to maintain concentration on content and stay on track during similar situations if you aren't prepared.

Knowing your material 100% makes the presentation easier, even when you are nervous, because you can focus on the delivery. Practice delivering the presentation over and over again, out loud, to help overcome the fear of forgetting what to say.

Visualize your success beforehand. If you are afraid you will stumble on the words, remember the message is what is important and don't hesitate to use a little self-deprecating humor if you get tongue tied. Remember too, a pause before you start speaking is a powerful way to draw the audience in and relieve you of the pressure to immediately start speaking.

One tip that can help you feel prepared is to have a 3x5 card ready with one or two relevant quotes on it. If you get completely lost and forget where you are, pull out the card, share the quote, and your thoughts. That will buy you some time to think and get yourself back on track. You won't have as much stage fright because you won't have to worry about not having anything to say.

Whenever it's possible, I try to meet some members of the audience before I speak. I usually don't get to meet everyone, and I probably wouldn't remember everyone's name even if I did. But, if I can meet some people and remember their names, I can more easily connect with the audience while I'm speaking. If I can reference them in my speech or speak directly to them, it's even more powerful.

When it comes to connecting with a crowd, nothing will turn them off like boring them with too much information. The rule of thumb that works for me is to share a story for each principle or lesson I'm teaching.

Make sure to use a variety of different stories. I like to include some funny ones because humor helps you connect with a crowd. We all enjoy laughing, so be sure to include some humor. This was difficult for me at first, and I spent a lot of time learning from other speakers who were funny.

As you speak, make eye contact with those in the audience. Don't stare at them endlessly, but stop and pause, look at someone while making a point. Then, move on to someone else. This will help them feel connected to you.

Connecting with a crowd isn't much different than connecting with one person – it's just on a much larger scale. Don't be afraid to show your emotions and let them feel your passion. Don't hesitate to let them know you care about them and want to help them.

It's important to be yourself because you won't feel comfortable trying to be anyone or anything else. If you aren't comfortable, your audience won't be either.

CHAPTER TWENTY SIX
BEING SOCIAL
WITH SOCIAL MEDIA

"What is interesting is the power and the impact of social media... So we must try to use social media in a good way."
~Malala Yousafzai

Not too long ago, books about communication wouldn't have needed a chapter about social media. Today however, 78% of Americans have a social media profile according to Statista. (Statista.com, The Statistics Portal of 18,000 studies and statistics)

Social media and the internet have transformed how we connect and communicate with people all around the globe.

I can remember when we didn't make a long distance phone call out of our area code because it was so expensive. These days, it's not unusual for me to Skype for hours with someone many thousands of miles away in France, Australia, England, and other places without any cost.

Social media has become a tool to reach thousands, or hundreds of thousands, of people who otherwise might have never heard of us or from us. Like any opportunity to influence people, it comes with great responsibility. On one hand, what you post can have positive influence. On the other, it could have negative influence.

The problem with social media is it's all too easy for us to see only the shiny parts of the lives of our "friends," contacts, and network. We see the vacation photos that look amazing, the first day of school pictures that are perfect, and the Pinterest perfect creations that are foolproof – until you try it. We may feel inferior when our life doesn't seem fun or exciting compared to the snapshots we see on Facebook.

Of course, the opposite happens sometimes too – where only the dark side is shared. Some people put too much on social media, making public their frustrations with their recently divorced ex-spouse or their lack of tolerance for other religious or political views. Perhaps, because it offers a feeling of anonymity, we sometimes feel free to express ourselves without considering the effects of our words. #NoFilter might sound like a great Instagram hash tag, but it's not really a good principle to base your social media comments on.

We must also realize some people appear to have a life that seems too good to be true – because it isn't true.

Some people can use social media for great harm by creating fake accounts, deceiving others, and spreading negative emotions.

How much to share on social media is a personal decision, and I can't answer that for everyone.

What I do want to point out is the need to be true to your values, even on social media. When people look at your profile and your posts, who do they see? Are you the same person on Facebook and Twitter that you are in church on Sunday morning?

If the answer is no, then it's time to do some soul searching and realize who we are on the inside is what others will see on the outside.

I worked for an organization that routinely checked social media profiles before hiring a candidate for a job. If the candidate appeared to be the same person on their social media account as they were in the job interview, they had nothing to worry about. However, if they were deceitful about something or if they simply appeared unprofessional and unqualified, it could hurt their chances of getting hired.

I once spoke to a large group of girls at a college sorority. One of the things I shared with them is that once you put something on the internet, it stays there forever. Even if you delete it later, it could still be out there because someone saw it and saved it. Or, it might sit on a remote server somewhere for years, but much like the words you say, you can't really take it back.

Who you are inside and what you value inside will naturally come out. I look at my Facebook posts from seven or eight years ago, and it appears I was mostly concerned with getting my homework done, exercising, getting my job done, and spending time with Mack. I'm not ashamed of that – those are exactly the things I valued back then, and I didn't have to work to hide them.

However, if you look at my social media posts today, you can tell I value being a positive influence on others. You will see leadership lessons, blogs, and positive quotes. You will also still see some posts about exercise and spending time with Mack. I still value those things, but I also value some new things.

What you will see from my social media is that I'm consistently the same person on social media that I am in real life.

I don't need a filter - I just need to make sure I value things that are principle-centered, because who we are sometimes is who we are all the time. It's okay to be transparent on social media. In fact, transparency and authenticity are something we don't have enough of. I'm not saying cover up who you are – I'm saying make sure you are a principle-centered person who is living in alignment with your moral compass and "practicing what you preach.

CHAPTER TWENTY SEVEN
USING HUMOR

"I love people who make me laugh. I honestly think it's the thing I like most, to laugh. It cures a multitude of ills. It's probably the most important thing in a person."

~Audrey Hepburn

Laughter is an important part of life. It's also an important part of connecting with others. A strong sense of humor and the ability to not take yourself, or anything else, too seriously is a great gift when it comes to communicating and connecting with others.

Using humor to connect with others wasn't always easy for me. I was not naturally quick witted. When I tried to force it, it came across as sarcastic. Sarcasm is not humor, and people are turned off by it. Avoid sarcasm if you truly want to connect with others.

I can't teach you everything you need to know about humor in this chapter. In fact, I can't teach you everything you need to know about humor period. I firmly believe you can get better at using humor, just like I did even if you aren't a naturally "funny" person. However, a large part of learning any new skill is doing it and learning by trial and error what works and what doesn't.

The benefit of using humor is found in raising emotional energy. Then, letting your powerful points hit home as you bring the emotional energy down. Whether you are talking to one person or one thousand, shifting the emotional energy will help you stay connected to your listeners. It keeps you from being boring. As Bill Gove pointed out, *"Sameness is the death of the speaker."*

If you naturally use humor already, you have a head start. If you don't, it's okay because you can learn.

Here are seven tips that have helped me:

1) **Don't try to be funny all the time.** One thing I have learned is humor works well when you aren't expecting it. Aristotle said, *"The secret to humor is surprise."* When you catch people off guard, they will be surprised and find themselves laughing. This goes back to my point about changing the emotional energy. Don't try to be funny all the time.

2) **Timing is important.** It's probably one of the most difficult things to explain and to learn, but timing is critical when it comes to humor. If you say it too early or too late, it falls flat.

3) **Make sure it's appropriate.** If you are speaking from the stage, make sure to do your research on your audience before using humor. Speaker Elizabeth McCormick regularly uses a funny statement about her "Starter husband" in her keynote. However, I heard her share once that she used the line at a women's event and no one laughed. Later, she realized they were a religious group that didn't believe in divorce, so they didn't appreciate her attempt at humor.

4) **Be Yourself.** I know I've said this in other chapters, but it's worth repeating – don't try to be someone else or to copy someone else. It's great to learn from others, but make sure you are always *you*. It's especially important when using humor. If you don't think something is funny, your audience won't either.

5) **Laugh at yourself.** Will Rogers said, *"Everything is funny, as long as it's happening to somebody else."* Let your listener(s) realize you don't take yourself too seriously. Give them permission to laugh with you, not just at you. Laughing at yourself brings humor without making anyone else feel silly or stupid. Laughter at someone else's expense may make some laugh, but the person who is the brunt of the joke probably won't appreciate it.

6) **Exaggerate – a little.** Be careful because you don't want to go over the top, but it can be a great way to get people laughing. You don't want to make something up - be sure your exaggeration is obviously an exaggeration. You could say, "I knew it was time to go buy groceries when I opened the fridge and only saw a stick of butter and a piece of cheese." Exaggeration can help create the image.

7) **Keep it clean.** This actually applies whether you are trying to be funny or not, but keep it clean. If you have to use profanity to make a point, don't make it. Honestly, the English language is very expressive and plenty colorful. There are many adjectives available if you will simply choose to learn them.

CHAPTER TWENTY EIGHT
PRACTICE MAKES BETTER

"Take advantage of every opportunity to practice your communication skills so that when important occasions arise, you will have the gift, the style, the sharpness, the clarity, and the emotions to affect other people."

~Jim Rohn

Much like learning to walk, there are some basic principles and practices that will help you learn to communicate and connect better. You have read quite a few in this book and perhaps others.

But, also like learning to walk, all the tips and tricks in the world won't help you unless they are applied. The only way to learn how, when, and where to apply them is by practicing.

You have heard the saying "Practice makes perfect," probably from your piano teacher, your football coach, or perhaps your parents.

I don't believe it. None of us are perfect – trust me, there is no such thing this side of heaven. Practice makes you better. Practice brings improvement. But, practice doesn't make perfect, especially when it comes to interacting with other people.

When we are communicating, we are going to get it wrong sometimes. The best thing you can do at that point is learn from the mistake and move on. Practice again. Then, practice some more.

And, no matter how much you practice, sometimes things will still come out wrong because people are different.

As I mentioned, Mack and I were part of a team of coaches training the leaders of Guatemala on leadership in 2013. We were in Guatemala for a week, and the team trained over 20,000 leaders on leadership principles. The theme for the week was "Transformation."

Our very first day there, John C. Maxwell met with the entire team and cast the vision for the week. We all went through training on the materials we would be teaching. During one of the breaks, Mack and I were given the opportunity to participate in the videoing of "A Minute with Maxwell," John's short leadership lessons that he shares daily.

In those lessons, John teaches for just a minute or two on one word and leadership principles related to that word. He does it completely unscripted and often has someone in the video with him choose the word. We were excited to have the opportunity to choose a word and have John teach on it. They would video us choosing the word and his teaching, all in front of the entire team of about 150 people.

Mack told me to choose the word, and I very carefully thought about it before selecting "Transparent." I thought it was a great word for a leadership lesson because leaders should be transparent.

I then realized it was very close to our theme word of "Transformation" and cautioned myself to remember to say the right word when the videoing started.

I mentally rehearsed what I was going to say several times, so I would feel confident and get it right. I concentrated very hard as we were called up front. I was determined not to mess up my word choice.

If you have never seen John speak, you can tell he is a very comfortable speaker. He is relaxed and calm while speaking because he has been speaking and teaching for over 40 years. He's also very comfortable with the leadership material he teaches. I was determined to come across as collected as he was.

As we walked up to stand with John, Mack whispered

to me, "I'm going to let you do all the talking."

"Uh, okay." I nodded, mentally adding into my rehearsed script that I needed to introduce us both.

The videoing started and John asked us to introduce ourselves and give him the word to teach on.

"Transparent….transparent…" I reminded myself just before speaking.

"Hello my name is *Mack* Story and our word for the day is Transparent." I breathed a sigh, glad I had remember the right word.

It took me a split second to realize I had just introduced myself as *Mack* instead of introducing him as Mack and myself as Ria.

It took everyone else just about that long too, and the entire room burst into laughter with me. I begged for a re-do and was very grateful to get it. I can laugh at my mistakes, but I certainly did not want to be known as the woman who forgot her name on the "Minute with Maxwell Bloopers."

I learned a great lesson. Practice makes you better, but not perfect. No matter how much we practice, we will still mess up sometimes. That's okay. The goal is to keep working at it and to keep improving.

Communication and connection skills can be improved – just like any other skill. It may come easier to some people than others. It certainly didn't come naturally to me. I've applied the lessons I've shared with you in this book. I have transformed my ability and confidence to connect and communicate with others in almost any environment or setting.

Easy? No. Quick? No. Worth it? YES!

CHAPTER TWENTY NINE
TELLING YOUR STORY

"If we think that this life is all there is to life, then there is no interpretation of our problems, our pain, not even of our privileges. But everything changes when we open up to the possibility that God's story is really our story too."

~Max Lucado

We all love stories. We love to be captivated by a story, whether it's funny, sad, or even romantic. They light up our emotions and fire up the imagination. They teach us so much because we can relate to them.

I shared my story at a women's ministry event recently. After I spoke, one of the ladies from the audience purchased my book, *Beyond Bound and Broken*, and said she is going to write her own book to help others. I was incredibly humbled to hear I had inspired her to share something she has been holding in for more than 20 years. She had been holding it in because she felt like a victim. When I shared my story, she realized she had a choice – see herself as a victim or as a survivor.

We never choose to become a victim. We must choose to become a survivor.

We all have a story to tell. We've all experienced things in life that have shaped us, molded us, refined us, or defined us. John Barth said, *"The story of your life is not your life. It is your story."*

Look at some who overcame incredible adversity: Les Brown, Liz Murray, Bethany Hamilton, and so many others. These are examples of people who have stories. They didn't let the story define them. They let it refine them. It's how we frame our story that determines whether we let it define the rest of our life or whether we let it refine the rest of our life.

Reframing allows one to choose to be a survivor

instead of a victim. Reframing our stories helps us realize we aren't victims at all but rather strong, resilient people who have been shaped by our experiences.

It's not the facts of our life that determine our hope for the future. It's what we tell *ourselves* about our stories that determines our hope for the future. Some people with painful stories see themselves as victims and feel the hand life dealt them was bad. Other people with painful stories choose to take inspiration from their story and make a difference in the lives of others.

Howard Schultz said, *"The reservoir of all my life experiences shaped me as a person and a leader."*

Reframing our stories into something positive creates the very foundation of leadership – leading oneself. It's the ability to influence ourselves that helps us overcome adversity in life and be resilient. If we can't lead ourselves, we won't be successful trying to lead or influence anyone else either.

If you don't reframe your story, you may let it define the rest of your life. If you can frame it, you can *reframe* it.

Find meaning and purpose from your past to create the future you want. There is more to telling your story than just sharing your history or what has happened to you so far on this journey we call life. It's not only about telling the story. It's about telling what you have learned from your story. Share how those experiences shaped you and made you better.

We all have stories. Stories of good times and bad times. Sad stories, happy stories, funny stories, and stories of redemption. Motivational speaker Les Brown said, *"You have a story. Someone needs to hear your story and only you can help that person."*

When I heard those words in 2013, they hit me hard, like a fast-moving truck. I knew I had a story. But, I didn't want to tell it.

How selfish of me.

I was holding back from helping someone else because I didn't want to share my story. I didn't want to talk about my pain, my scars, my shame, or even my redemption. I didn't want to be vulnerable.

It took six months for me to realize my story isn't about me. In fact, it's really not even my story. It's God's story, told through my life. When I realized that, I found the strength and courage to share my story. In doing so, I broke down the prison walls in my heart that I had spent years building. And, I began helping others break down their walls too.

That's the strength of sharing our stories. But, don't just tell the story. Share the lessons learned from it. Share your purpose, your passion, and yes, even your pain.

Once you have crossed the chasm and come through chaos, you have the opportunity of a lifetime. The opportunity to turn around and throw a rope to help someone else cross over safely too. When you are vulnerable, you will find strength. That's the strength of your story.

Today, I tell my story to help and inspire others. I also help and inspire others to learn to tell their own stories.

There might only be one person who needs to hear your story. Or, the whole world might need to hear it. When we share our stories, we create a ripple effect that touches lives in a way we may never know. Each and every day, I hear from someone who has heard my story. They tell me how I've touched their life.

My story isn't about me. Your story isn't about you. Our story is about helping someone else realize they too can overcome. That power is in your story.

CHAPTER THIRTY
FREQUENTLY ASKED QUESTIONS

"I never learn anything talking. I only learn things when I ask questions."

~Lou Holtz

Much of the material in this book came through my own reading and learning over the years. I've shared what has worked for me and what hasn't worked for me. I've included points that answer many of the questions others have asked me about communication and connection over the years. This topic is one Mack and I speak on often. We offer training classes and keynote speeches on Effective Communication. We even teach a class for couples on communication and connection (or Leadership in Relationships) called "Two Become One."

I also want to share the answers to a few "Frequently Asked Questions." These may be questions you still have after reading this book or some things I didn't address that you may not have thought about. I'm sure you have heard there are no "dumb" questions, but you may not have heard there may be more than one "right" answer.

Remember, communication and connection is often subjective or situational, so rather than applying the practices related to connecting, make sure you apply the principles. Principles (for example, listening first to understand the other person), work in every situation, while practices (for example, introducing yourself by shaking hands) only work in some situations.

1) **How do I communicate a mission and vision to my team?** This is a tough issue for almost every organization. I think it boils down to one question – does your mission or vision clearly articulate your organizational "Why?" Your

mission or vision should be crystal clear about the purpose of your company. Why you and your team are doing what they do matters more than anything. Simon Sinek has a terrific TEDx talk and a book called "Start With Why." I highly recommend every person and every organization consider their stated mission in light of Simon's outline of "Why/How/What." Customers and team members don't buy-in to what you do. They buy-in to why you do it.

2) **How do I organize and articulate my thoughts during a presentation?** For me, I find it best to clearly outline my thoughts *before* the presentation and create a brief bulleted list on a single sheet or even a 5"x7" card. Clarifying my points beforehand helps me flow smoothly through them and having them in front of me gives me a quick reference to fall back on if I get off track. If I'm using notes, I don't try to hide it. I may even say, "Let me check my notes and make sure I'm covering everything." Above all, be prepared and know your material.

3) **What do I do when someone is not really listening to me?** You will know when someone "checks out" of your conversation, just like they know when you check out. When this happens, I usually offer space. "I can tell this isn't a good time, or you have something else on your mind. Can we finish this discussion later?" Or, "I would love to discuss this more when we can both focus better. I know you are busy now, would this afternoon work?" That way, you are

acknowledging (understanding) they aren't engaged, asking permission to continue when they are engaged, and not making a big deal of it. Usually what happens is the person will check back in and give you permission to continue right then.

4) **What can I do when someone is not responding to a time sensitive request?** Remember, we can only work on ourselves. If this happens, the first thing is to make sure you clearly communicated the expectations or requirements up front. If the answer is no, then you've got an opportunity to improve in this area by communicating more clearly next time. If the answer is yes, there are two possible reasons they aren't responsive: 1) The person is aware of the need, but is overwhelmed or overcommitted; or 2) You aren't a priority in their world. You may or may not be able to do much about the first reason beyond asking for clarification about when you can expect a response. The latter reason means you have an opportunity to improve your connection and influence with that person. The issue may have started before you even made the request, so you may have to go back to the beginning to start building the relationship. However, it will be well worth it.

5) **How can I communicate expectations?** This comes down to being simple with your communication. Talking to someone on their level is critical. For example, if the expectation is for your child to clean their room, make sure you

have communicated what "clean" looks like, in language they can understand. If possible, ask for feedback, so you know they understand. Focus on clear and concise statements. Remember, if you can't define it simply, you can't explain it simply.

6) **What if I'm trying to connect with someone, but they think I am being manipulative?** We see the world as we are, not as it is. If you aren't trying to manipulate someone, but they believe you are, odds are good they often attempt to manipulate others. The other possibility is they are questioning your "why" or your own motivation in doing something. They may not feel like you care. They may be asking, is this about mutual benefit or your benefit? First, establish clearly you care, and you aren't trying to manipulate. It's all about trust. Communicate your reason and the "why" behind it until they are certain of it. Then, and only then, can you move forward. Also, refer back to chapter nine.

7) **How can I make sure all the details are communicated?** It's a challenge we all face as we become more experienced. We forget the beginner's mindset of simply not knowing what we don't know. If you have ever tried to teach someone a completely new skill, you realize just how much you unconsciously know and do, without thinking about it. To overcome this, especially in the workplace, it helps to take the time to slow down and walk through something, one slow step at a time. Don't assume everyone

knows everything. Explain even the little details as you go. Make sure you allow them to ask you questions. If possible, have them explain what they heard back to you, so you will know if the message was clearly received. I also think it helps to learn something new yourself on a regular basis, so you can empathize, relative to what it feels like to not know everything.

8) **How can I communicate/connect with someone who is working remotely away from me?** Long distance connection and communication has come a long way, however technology brings its own challenges and opportunities. I can't answer every scenario here, so I'll simply say it's best to ask yourself this question every time you get ready to interact with someone long distance. "How can I connect with Bob before we talk about work during our Skype session today?" Or, "What can I say in this email to clearly communicate my concern for Sally's sick child?" Keep in mind, Emoticons were invented because written words often don't communicate the depth of feeling in the manner that spoken words do. If something is sensitive, pick up the phone and talk or meet face to face if at all possible, instead of using email. It takes longer, but it's far better in terms of communication and connection. Sometimes, we must go slow to go fast.

ABOUT THE AUTHOR

Like many, Ria faced adversity in life. Raised on an isolated farm in Alabama, she was sexually abused by her father from age 12 – 19. Desperate to escape, she left home at 19 without a job, a car, or even a high school diploma. Ria learned to be resilient, not only surviving, but thriving. She worked her way through college, earning her MBA with a cumulative 4.0 GPA, and had a successful career in the corporate world of administrative healthcare.

Ria's background includes more than 10 years in administrative healthcare with several years in management including Director of Compliance and Regulatory Affairs for a large healthcare organization. Ria's responsibilities included oversight of thousands of organizational policies, organizational compliance with all State and Federal regulations, and responsibility for several million dollars in Medicare appeals.

Today, Ria is a motivational leadership speaker and author of 9 books. Ria was selected three times to speak on stage at International John Maxwell Certification Events. Motivational speaker Les Brown also invited Ria to share the stage with him in Los Angeles, CA. Ria and her husband, Mack Story, co-founded Top Story Leadership which offers motivational speaking, leadership training, coaching, and consulting.

ABOUT MACK STORY

Mack began his career in manufacturing on the front lines of a machine shop. He grew himself into upper management and found his niche in lean manufacturing and along with it, developed his passion for leadership.

With more than 20 years working with and on the front lines, he brings a powerful blend of practical experience and leadership knowledge to his clients. Mack is a published author of several leadership books including: Blue-Collar Leadership, Blue-Collar Leadership & Supervision, Defining Influence, 10 Values of High Impact Leaders, MAXIMIZE Your Potential, MAXIMIZE Your Leadership Potential, Change Happens, and more.

He understands that everything rises and falls on leadership.

For more detailed information on Mack, please visit TopStoryLeadership.com.

READ MORE BOOKS BY RIA

The Effective Leadership Series books are written to develop and enhance your leadership skills while also helping you increase your abilities in areas like communication and relationships, time management, planning and execution, and leading and implementing change. Look for more books in the Effective Leadership Series:

- *Straight Talk: The Power of Effective Communication*
- *Change Happens: Leading Yourself and Others through Change*
- *PRIME Time: The Power of Effective Planning*
- *Leadership Gems: 30 Characteristics of Very Successful Leaders*
- *Leadership Gems for Women: 30 Characteristics of Very Successful Women*

One of the greatest leadership myths is that you must be a "born" leader to be successful. In truth, leadership and influence are skills that can be developed and improved. However, to be very successful, you must intentionally develop your skills, so you can lead and influence others at work, in your career, at home, church, or even as a volunteer.

In *Leadership Gems*, Ria has packed 30 precious gems of leadership wisdom on characteristics of very successful leaders - and insight on how you can develop them yourself. These lessons will help you become a very successful leader regardless of whether you are in a formal leadership position or not.

READ MORE BOOKS BY RIA

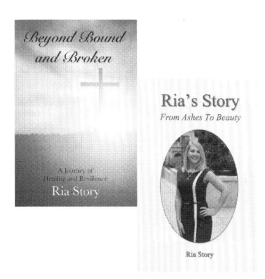

In *Beyond Bound and Broken*, Ria shares how she overcame shame, fear, and doubt stemming from years of being sexually abused by her father. Forced to play the role of a wife and even shared with other men due to her father's perversions, Ria left home at 19 without a job, a car, or even a high-school diploma. This book contains lessons on resilience and overcoming adversity that you can apply in your own life.

In *Ria's Story From Ashes To Beauty*, Ria tells her story of growing up as a victim of sexual abuse from age 12 – 19, and leaving home to escape. She shares how she went on to thrive and learn to help others by sharing her story.

READ MORE BOOKS BY RIA

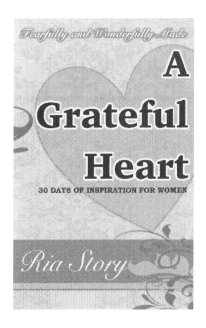

Become inspired by this 30-day collection of daily devotions for women, where you will find practical advice on intentionally living with a grateful heart, inspirational quotes, short journaling opportunities, and scripture from God's Word on practicing gratitude.

READ BOOKS BY MACK STORY

Blue-Collar Leadership and *Blue-Collar Leadership and Supervision* are written specifically for those on the front lines of the Blue-Collar workforce and those who lead them. With 30 short, easy to read chapters, the *Blue-Collar Leadership Series* books contain powerful leadership lessons in a simple and easy to understand format.

Visit www.BlueCollarLeaders.com to learn more, get your free download of the first five chapters from both books, and watch Mack's video related video series.

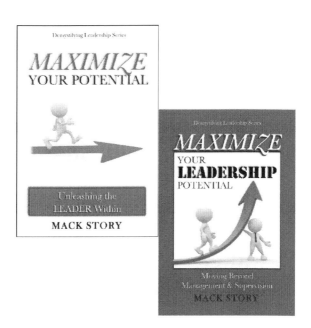

Mack's *MAXIMIXE Your Potential* and *MAXIMIZE Your Leadership Potential* books are the white-collar version of the *Blue-Collar Leadership Series*. These books are written specifically for those working on the front lines and those who lead them. With 30 short, easy to read chapters, they contain powerful leadership lessons in a simple and easy to understand format.

Everything rises and falls on influence. Nothing will impact your professional and personal life more than your ability to influence others. Are you looking for better results in your life, team, or organization? In *Defining Influence*, everyone at all levels will learn the keys to intentionally increasing your influence in all situations from wherever you are.

READ BOOKS BY MACK STORY

It's no longer "Buyer Beware!" It's "Seller Beware!" Why? Today, the buyer has the advantage over the seller. Most often, they are holding it in their hand. It's a smart phone. They can learn everything about your product before they meet you. The major advantage you do still have is: YOU!

This book is filled with 30 short chapters providing unique insights that will give you the advantage, not over the buyer, but over your competition: those who are selling what you're selling. It will help you sell yourself.

READ BOOKS BY MACK STORY

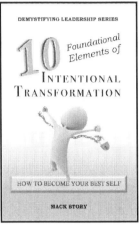

The *10 Values of High Impact Leaders* will help you lead with speed and develop 360° of influence from wherever you are. High impact leaders align their habits with key values in order to maximize their influence.

10 Foundational Elements of Intentional Transformation is a "how-to" roadmap of transformation. The principles Mack shares in this book are the principles he personally applied to transform his life, his career, and his relationships, both personally and professionally.

Top Story Leadership
Powerful Leadership - Simplified

- ➤ Certified Speakers and Trainers
- ➤ Published Authors – 19 books available on leadership and inspirational topics
- ➤ Custom Leadership Programs

Keynote Speaking and Training:

Leadership Development/Personal Growth
Organizational Change/Transformation
Communication/Trust/Relationships
Time Management/Planning/Execution

Engage, Educate, and Empower
Your Audience or Team!

"Mack and Ria understand people! The dynamic team made such an impact on our front line supervision that they were begging for more training! We highly recommend Mack and Ria!" Rebecca, Director Process Improvement, GKN

"We would highly recommend Mack and Ria as speakers...their presentation was inspirational, thought-provoking, and filled with humor. They taught us some foundational leadership principles." Stephen, President-elect, WCR

TopStoryLeadership.com
Email: info@TopStoryLeadership.com

52263656R00078

Made in the USA
Columbia, SC
03 March 2019